WHAT OTHERS SAY ABOUT THE BOOK

There is hardly any more urgent path to take in the world today than the one Nharrel and his family have taken: the path of wholehearted obedience to God in missionary service among the unreached and least reached. He models for the reader what it means to give one's life over wholly to a missionary calling yet feel all the while abundantly blessed. If it were not for pioneer missionaries like him, who obey God's call to go where Christ is least known or unknown, then my own family would still be living in darkness.

These are also stories of prayer, the glowing ember that is always found at the core of all mission impact, and the engine behind all mission endeavours. May the Lord of the Harvest use these remarkable tales to call more into his harvest fields!

—Dr Joshua Bogunjoko, International Director of SIM

This collection of stories educates, inspires, and challenges the reader. Often, we learn best through stories like these frontline accounts from the field. Told from the perspective of the emerging missionary force from the non-Western world, they are a foretaste of what we might expect in global missions.

—Dr Ted Esler, President of Missio Nexus

Research often tells us statistics of how Christianity is growing rapidly in the continent of Africa. But how is God building his church on the continent? Through carefully narrated stories from Kamukuland, Nigeria, our brother Nharrel opens for us a small window to see the work of the Holy Spirit in Nigeria and in Africa. These stories sounded like they were written about the rural village where I was born and raised in Ethiopia. You will be intrigued by the faith and faithfulness of missionaries and local believers to boldly proclaim the gospel no matter what.

—Dr Bekele Shanko,
Global Vice President of Campus Crusade for Christ,
President of GACX (a global alliance for church multiplication)

The book calls our attention to God's awesome power to rescue a people group from bondage to ancestral worship, traditions, cultural practices, and the wicked spirits and evil gods that had held them captive for many years. What can be more convincing of genuine transformation than the fact that some characters in these stories are now themselves missionaries to other people groups? This book is a timely message to the church, especially people who are ashamed of the gospel because they have not yet seen it as "the power of God at work, saving everyone who believes" (Romans 1:16).

Well-written, precise, and very practical, this book does not present a set of doctrines or theories on how to do evangelism and church planting, but Nharrel's life experiences on the mission field. The book presents testimonies of God's power to provide, heal, deliver from demonic forces, miraculously answer prayers, and defend those who depend on him. The book is a must-read for all serving missionaries and missions and church administrators, and a great asset for pastors, teachers, and all Christians.

—Prof Ezekiel Oluyemi Odebunmi, Former National Chairman of Calvary Ministries (CAPRO) Nigeria, Professor of Chemistry at University of Ilorin

Concise, simple, and deeply insightful, this book is a faith-induced spiritual goldmine. These stories are proof that God can do extraordinary things through and among ordinary people. Simple prayers offered in faith bring about life-changing results. We sometimes forget this as we get carried away by big grammar, logic, and showmanship.

A guide for anyone looking to grow their faith in Christ, this book also offers revival and renewal for those who have become faint in their walk with God. Reflections and thought-provoking questions at the end of each chapter make the book a valuable resource for deeper Scripture engagement. The transformative power of the gospel is captured in this powerful reminder: God is still in the business of performing miracles for his glory through obedient missionaries. In times like these when Christians are faced with persecution in Nigeria and around the world, this book should be welcomed with two hands and an obedient heart!

—Rev Dr Gideon Para-Mallam, Global Mission Leader and Peace Advocate in Jos, Nigeria

Three things stand out as I reflect on these stories of God's power, faithfulness, and grace in Kamukuland. First, church planting is not a routine or programmed process. Among peoples who have been held in bondage by the evil one for centuries, the words of the gospel have been accompanied by power (1 Thessalonians 1:5). God's Spirit sometimes works like the wind (John 3:8) in people's hearts drawing them out of darkness into the Light. Other times, God's work is like leaven (Luke 13:20-21) in a community, transforming it over decades. When we look back, we are amazed at all he has done. And third, God is preparing the African church to take their place on the global stage as the next generation of Great Commission workers, taking the gospel to hard and hostile peoples and places, and re-evangelizing the West in the lands that sent missionaries to them in the first place! May it be so!

—Dr Jerry Todd Lafferty,
Executive VP of the International Mission Board

In his very readable but deeply insightful style, Nharrel takes us behind the curtain to see what a modern African's cross-cultural missionary life and work look like, and at the same time to challenge us to childlike faith. Thanks, my "running mate" for how you serve the church with your writing gift. I pray I catch up soon.

—Chimezie Onyebilanma, former National Director of Calvary Ministries (CAPRO) South Africa, host of Chim's Talk Africa on Trinity Broadcasting Network

The message of Jesus has always been carried by testimonies. We've experienced his authority over sickness, demons, sin, divorce, snakes, poison, and our greatest enemy death, and we want to tell the world about it! These things show that God is with us and all authority in heaven and earth has been given to him – and people everywhere in Jerusalem, Judea, Samaria, Kamukuland, Europe, America, and the "ends of the earth" should recognize him as King.

These stories from Kamukuland are told here by a master storyteller and expert writer. Read them to your family and friends and be inspired to see the great things that the Lord can do among us if we will only trust him.

—Prof Andy Warren-Rothlin, Translation Consultant for United Bible Societies Switzerland

This book stands in its own class. It is a compilation of true stories from the mission field, but ultimately, it is not about the author, his team, nor the church in Kamukuland. It is about our God. It bears incredible evidence that our God is real, alive, ever faithful, a mighty man of battle, and has all the powers in heaven and on earth. He has given Nharrel the grace to write this book for the glory of his name, the edification of believers, and the strengthening of his church. I commend this book to all believers, trusting in the Holy Spirit's power to transform our lives as we meditate on the heart-thrilling synopsis of God's mighty acts.

—Prof Adesegun Fatusi,
Vice Chancellor of the University of Medical Sciences, Ondo, Nigeria

These stories may seem like fairy tales, but they are real. For instance, I was personally involved in the encounter with the Kamuku gods, which may seem exaggerated, but not even half of what transpired has been captured. Read this book and you will come to know that little faith exercised in prayer to God through Jesus Christ changes situations.

—Rev Samson D. Mancha, Former CAPRO Missionary Colleague,
now Pastor and Lecturer with Church of Christ in Nations (COCIN)

This is one of the most open, honest, and truly earnest books that you can read to encourage your faith in Christ Jesus. The faith of these simple people, narrated in this book, moved mountains in their various communities. Read this exceptional masterpiece and your life will not remain the same.

—Dr Mary Erasmus Sulai,
Associate Professor at Gombe State University, Nigeria

Such an enriching and fascinating read.

—Yetunde Omodia,
Missionary and Former Missionary Colleague in Kamukuland

NAMANI J. NHARREL

I'D RATHER DIE ON THE HIGH GROUND

GRIPPING STORIES OF TRIUMPH OVER THE POWERS OF DARKNESS AND PERSECUTION FROM A NIGERIAN MISSION FIELD

INSIGHT BOOKS
AFRICAN ISSUES AFRICA'S AUTHORS

OASIS INTERNATIONAL PUBLISHING

I'd Rather Die on the High Ground

ISBN 13: 978-1-59452-863-7
ISBN: 1-59452-863-2

Published by Oasis International Ltd, in partnership with Namani J. Nharrel, based on his first edition, titled *Encouraged by Their Faith*. To find out more about Calvary Ministries (CAPRO), visit capromissions.org.

Oasis International is a ministry devoted to growing discipleship through publishing African voices.

- We *engage* Africa's most influential, most relevant, and best communicators for the sake of the gospel.
- We *cultivate* local and global partnerships in order to publish and distribute high-quality books and Bibles.
- We *create* contextual content that meets the specific needs of Africa, has the power to transform individuals and societies, and gives the church in Africa a global voice.

Oasis is: *Satisfying Africa's Thirst for God's Word.* For more information, go to oasisinternational.com.

Printed in India.

23 24 25 26 27 28 29 30 31 32 BPI 10 9 8 7 6 5 4 3 2 1

In memory of Baba Sata Maikujeri, Baba Dogo, and Baba Bulus Bobi.

These men were among the first Kamuku believers who followed Christ through the ministry of the American missionary, the Reverend L. E. Tuller, who worked in Kamukuland from the 1920s through the 1950s. I met these wonderful men of faith in the late 1990s while in Kamuku. They were a real encouragement to us later missionaries and to the young believers from our work. They have all now joined the presence of the Lord.

CONTENTS

Foreword 1

Encouraged by Their Faith 5

Present Day: Standing Strong 9

1. We Want a Zinc Roof 13
2. His Ways, Not Ours 22
3. Difficult Issues in Discipleship 29
4. A Preacher, Not a Patient 40
5. Are You Going Mad? 50
6. For This, He Must Die 59
7. I'd Rather Die on the High Ground 71
8. Like Magic, the Bees Disappeared 77
9. It Is Good Jesus Came for Koba 84
10. I Am for Jesus until Death 93
11. They Cast Out Demons 102
12. Authority over Snakes 111
13. When He Drinks a Deadly Poison 123
14. Brought before Kings 134
15. A Church of Missionaries 147

Your Prayers Can Make a Difference 151

Letter to a Young Missionary 155

Acknowledgements 159

FOREWORD

I am so excited that my brother, Nharrel, has decided to write this book of testimonies, and I am excited for several reasons.

Firstly, I have been so burdened that we are not capturing enough stories of what God is doing in the African missionary movements. It is sad to say that in many history, theological, and missiological classes, we still only refer to the exploits and testimonies of Western missionaries. While these stories are important points of reference, the time has come to include the stories of missionaries in and from Africa. God has been doing amazing things through African missionaries, but these are not being documented or utilized to nurture and mobilize new generations of missions and church leaders. God is also raising new armies of spiritual disciples from hitherto unreached people groups, but their stories are also not being captured. I am excited that brother Nharrel has chosen to take the bull by the horns to promote some of these yet untold testimonies, to the glory of God.

Another reason why I am excited about this book is because it captures the essence of faith transferring from one generation and people to the next. While most of the stories told are of what local believers did, we must not forget that their faith was woven intricately connected to what these believers saw and heard from their disciple-makers. Missions is only sustainable when the next generation of believers have "imbibed and embraced" the priorities, passions, and pursuits of their spiritual parents or leaders.

As a ministry, CAPRO emphasizes the centrality of Christ in doctrine and followership. We do not patronize fellow humans; neither do we venerate them nor make them the hub for any work of God. We see Christ and present Christ for who he truly is, "the champion who initiates and perfects our faith" (Hebrews 12:2). However, we also strongly believe in the ministry of discipleship and disciple-making. One of the biggest ailments in today's church is that people are following people who are not following Christ. From this book, we see the faith of people who learned it from those they followed, because their disciple-makers were Christ-focused.

A third reason I am excited about this book is because of the sincerity and openness with which it is written. Missionaries are not painted here as superhuman; in fact, our human limitations are sometimes displayed in the stories. We do not always have ready answers. We do not always have faith to move mountains. But this book is ultimately not about the power and wonder of missionaries or local believers. This book is about the faithfulness of God working through human vessels. The miracles showcased here are for Christ.

This is also not just a book of testimonies; it is a book that shows the unpredictability of pioneer ministries. It displays raw, unedited expressions of doubt, struggle, faith, and victory. Missionary work does not follow a precise plan from any textbook. Working with indigenous believers is always a walk of faith, of depending on God to provide wisdom in making God-honouring decisions. More importantly, it is exciting to see God developing genuine faith encounters with indigenous peoples. This book is a display of God's work in our brothers and sisters who joined our common faith, through God's work in us.

In conclusion, our hope and prayer is that our spiritual heirs shall indeed become greater than us. In missionary work, this is more acute as we sincerely and earnestly desire to see God work through the next generation of indigenous believers more than he worked through us. We know that God is always at work, but there is no greater pleasure than seeing God become the God of the next generation of believers among a people who had no believers. Having worked myself in the interior of Northern Nigeria, the Sudan, and the Middle East – and having left behind me footprints that continue to grow in the work of God in those places – I thank God for his mercies that keep raising up people of faith after the pioneer missionaries have moved on. The stories captured in this book are repeated thousands of times around the world. God revealed his plan to raise communities of believers among all the people groups around the world. To make this happen, the miracle of faith is a daily miracle happening in the hearts of people of faith – old and new. We continue to stand in awe and wonder of God, amazed by what he has done and is doing. This book is a glimpse into the faithfulness of God, with Brother Nharrel as God's point man taking us on the tour.

Dr Chinedu Conrad Oranye
Director, Partnerships & Resource Development
International Office, Calvary Ministries (CAPRO), Lagos, Nigeria

ENCOURAGED BY THEIR FAITH

Are you looking for a book that can carry you far from the mundane realities of your Christian faith, and immerse you in a world of dangerous and distant mission fields where missionaries, by their great faith, win countless souls to Christ, outwit the schemes of the Devil, and perform many miraculous exploits? If this is the type of book you are looking for, then allow me to warn you on no uncertain terms: this is not the book for you.

For these stories are not about the great feats of missionaries like myself, but about the great faith of new believers. These new believers courageously turned from idolatry to Jesus Christ. They accepted the message of salvation with simple faith. And when the need arose to put their faith into action, they did, and God honoured their "innocent" faith. The outcome marvelled even those of us missionaries who taught them. Our faith was encouraged by the faith of these young converts.

Are you living in a complicated and barren Christianity today? Do the Christian activities of church or group Bible studies feel routine and burdensome? Is reading the Word something you must force yourself to do or has praying become like talking to yourself?

Perhaps you wish you could find someone to teach you deep and amazing things about the Christian faith which you have followed for years, perhaps decades. But who is qualified to be your guide into deeper territories of faith that you may have heard about, but never experienced? Is there a minister of the gospel with years of pastoral experience who could show you something new? Perhaps the head of a multi-national ministry, or a theologian and author of some groundbreaking Christian book? Of course, there are the inspiring biographies of missionaries who have gone before – perhaps they are the ones who can teach you more than you now know.

But I would like to introduce you to a different guide, a very unlikely teacher. In this book you will find fellow pilgrims on the path to heaven who you might overlook in your search for a mentor in the faith. They are people living in a place you have never heard of, and they had only been Christians for a short time when these stories happened. Yet I believe they can teach you, as they did me, new and marvellous things. These are the people of Kamukuland.

What is it like to journey out of the bondage of traditional religions, ancestor worship, and oppression by evil spirits and into new faith in Jesus? The obstacle is not some intellectual conviction about whether God and the spirit world exist. They know this to be so. But the Kamuku people were afraid of abandoning idols which represent demons. Magiro, a god worshipped by a men's cult, used to mete out discipline to community members for perceived errors. Women who did not meet the demands of *Sarauniya* were often inflicted with suffering, sickness, poverty, and even death. Despite the danger, Kamuku believers encountered another spiritual power and trusted that Jesus was stronger and provided more protection.

Religion is closely tied to culture. It provides its adherents with their worldview, identity, social life, customs, and sense of belonging. The Kamuku disciples had to renounce aspects of their identities linked to the culture of idol worship, to take on unknown identities as Christian Kamuku. For an agnostic-turned-Christian to displace their leisure pursuits on Sundays for church involvement is not the same bold risk as displacing Magiro worship for church involvement. Yet this is what new Kamuku believers bravely did.

And even after they chose Jesus Christ, they, like the new churches in the book of Acts, encountered cultural dilemmas, the ever-present relationship challenges, and diverse opinions among Christians themselves. They grappled with these as new believers, rose to these occasions, and matured.

I urge you to read and learn from them that the Living God is alive indeed, that he honours our faith in action, that he hears the earnest prayers of his children, and that he extends his great power to move in the affairs of those who put their trust in him.

The faith of these ordinary people seen in action was exhibited in ordinary day-to-day living. No special announcements, no advertisements, no preparatory prayer meetings, and no calls for special days of prayer and fasting in most cases. Situations arose that needed divine intervention. The people had learned and knew that the God of their new faith controlled all situations. They approached him in prayer. He responded by overturning situations in their favour. All of this was for the glory of God and the expansion of his kingdom among a people who are predominantly non-Christians.

In telling these stories, I wish to reaffirm that prayers prayed in faith and in the name of the Lord Jesus will change situations. The stories here demonstrate that God still performs miracles in our time. They do not always occur in dramatic ways, but they surely occur in answer to the passionate prayers of those who pray believing God for the unusual. And when the miracles happen, they defy natural explanations.

The people of Kamukuland have also encouraged me to believe that the power – which protected in times of danger, provided in times of need, healed in times of sickness, cast out demons in times of oppression, comforted the wounded in spirit, overcame sinful habits, and above all, transformed lives – is real. That same power is available to all who put their trust in the Lord Jesus Christ today.

I'd Rather Die on the High Ground is a collection of stories about people who once lived in spiritual darkness, but when the Light came to them, they greeted it and obeyed it. The cast of ordinary characters here would be surprised to find themselves in the pages of a book, yet it is their ordinariness that helps us see ourselves in their lives and reveals the power of God through them. Neither their ordinariness nor yours stands in opposition to having great faith and living a life that can be used of God to transform a community and bring great glory to him.

The stories in *I'd Rather Die on the High Ground* are set in the Kamuku mission field of Calvary Ministries (known popularly as CAPRO), Niger State, Nigeria. The stories cover only part of the work of CAPRO in Kamukuland for part of the time I served there as a missionary field leader. Those whose stories are told were members of the local church that I and others planted and nurtured directly. Therefore, this is a book of a few stories of faith from a small church in one mission field.

Many mission stories and biographies have been written by authors from the West from a Western worldview. This has led to the popular misconception in some quarters that only Westerners are missionaries. Many people don't know there are African missionaries with equally gripping stories to tell the Christian world. Here is an attempt to tell the story of God and what he is doing through an African missionary.

Putting these short stories together has been with great fear in my heart. One fear is that of appearing to missionary colleagues to be blowing one's trumpet. Another is that others may have witnessed more daring exhibitions of faith in their works. They might ask, "What is that in comparison with what we have experienced?" I would reply, "Not much!"

I also feared the book may be coming out too soon. What if the characters do not last in the faith? But it has now been 20 years. Even if the persons or churches were no longer standing strong today, does this invalidate the stories? Not at all. After all, the apostle Paul ministered to some churches that fell to other religions long ago. But what Paul wrote to them and about them remains relevant to Christians of other places and later times.

I write because I was part of the events – true and verifiable stories that did not take place in secret – and I feel they can encourage more believers if only they are told. The truth is that I am just amazed at the wonder of teaching people to live by faith in principle, but in practice I had to learn the same faith from the same people whom I taught.

Read and be encouraged by their faith.

Namani J. Nharrel

PRESENT DAY
STANDING STRONG

One fateful day in March 2020, the church elders of various people groups reported to CAPRO's Hausa School of Missions to begin a two-month training. The school trained people to become missionaries in cross-cultural ministries among Hausa-speaking communities in Northern Nigeria and beyond, but we also held short-term refresher courses such as this one to develop the leadership of churches planted by CAPRO. The Kamuku team arrived late in the evening.

Early the next morning, there was a knock on my door. I opened it to a Kamuku man who reported, "Armed men invaded and abducted teachers and pupils of the Tuller Boarding Primary School in Maruba last night."

I was shaken, but I had to compose myself. I had dual roles in leading them. As the rest of this book recounts, over 20 years prior God used me to bring some of them to Christ as a missionary church planter in Kamukuland, so the Kamuku believers saw me as their team's "father". But now I also had the role of principal of the school where they had come for a refresher course.

Soon I would learn the fuller story, that a large number of bandits had invaded the school, shot a male staff member in the leg, and abducted eight teachers and one male pupil of the school. The school was closed.

The abducted staff and the pupil were held captives for 52 days before their release. The bandits returned two more times to the school to see if people were still there. On their last visit, they vandalised the property.

MORE ATTACKS

From that time, Kamukuland and neighbouring indigenous people groups of northwest Nigeria came under a series of deadly attacks from terrorists.

At first, the bandits came for livestock. They carted away herds of cattle, goats, sheep, and poultry as they went marauding from one location to another. They moved in droves with the seized animals, killing anyone who resisted them. A church member from Anguwan Citama was killed in such a raid.

After they had carried off most of the animals, it seemed as if the terrorists returned for the people. In April 2021, two church members were taken in the night from Anguwan Buba. One was a trainee in the School of Missions I headed. He went on break and was to return to school three days before he was abducted at gunpoint. The two men spent three days with the bandits before making their escape.

Throughout 2021 and 2022, many Kamuku villages were raided. People were injured, killed, and kidnapped. Houses were burnt. Food supplies and animals belonging to the people were carted away by the terrorists.

Sometime during 2021 and 2022, nearly all the Kamuku people in remote villages, especially in the areas where we worked, fled their homes to find refuge in nearby towns for fear of terrorist raids. A missionary who worked in Kamuku reported, "Most of the villagers, including our church members, are now scattered to different places. Some are camped with well-wishers in nearby towns, with everyone struggling to survive."

"TAKE UP YOUR CROSS . . ."

The people's means of livelihood is greatly affected by these deadly attacks. Subsistence farming is often their sole source of income, but they are unable to plant their crops or the plants. Terrorists have set fire to guinea corn fields waiting to be harvested. In some places, the villagers are forced to pay fines to the bandits to access their farms. Consequently, the people are in great lack of both food to feed themselves and money to meet other basic needs.

Church planting has been affected as well. As in other places of our work in northern Nigeria, most missionaries have been forced out of their mission stations. Those who stayed in some of the flash-point locations are targeted for kidnapping for ransom. Security concerns have prevented us from visiting as often as we wished to encourage them. Several missionaries with CAPRO and other mission agencies have been gruesomely murdered.

The churches the missionaries left behind are facing harsh times. For example, 11 out of the 13 local churches from our work in Kamuku are displaced and scattered. The remaining two live in fear and uncertainty.

Non-Christians are also affected by these acts of terrorism. In one of the several attacks on Ukuru, the raiders abducted more than 100 non-Christians, mainly women and children, after fierce resistance from the men. Their houses and property were burnt.[1]

In November 5, 2022, bandits abducted nine people, six Christians and three others from Angwan Tanko, one of the stations where we had worked. As a ransom, the bandits asked for more money than the whole village combined would have seen in their lives. If all their possessions were sold, the proceeds would not add up to the demanded amount.

We praise God that all were released on December 15, 2022, but it came at great expense. They sold their farm produce to pay the renegotiated and much reduced ransom. Such a dire situation is not uncommon. Pray with us for God to provide for their food needs and for a means to farm in the future.

HOPE

Anytime I hear of an attack on the Kamuku people, my heart bleeds in grief, like a mother watching her children being battered by bullies but

1 At the end of the book, I share my take on some motivations for the terrorism, only some of which can be termed religious persecution.

helpless to protect them. Yet I also remember my fears of 20 years ago, when I began writing this book. As I collected the stories of believers in Kamukuland, I wondered, "What if the believers I have written about do not last in the faith? What if they scatter to the winds?"

My heart fills again with praise and joy as I see how, in the midst of their great losses, the believers have not lost their faith in Christ. Though they are scattered, they are rooted strongly in the faith we delivered to them more than 20 years ago.

The believers who find themselves in the same location meet to worship and pray together. One such community recently held a week-long prayer and fasting time. The primary school that was attacked continued in a different location and is managed by the Kamuku people, including some who are graduates of the same school. The believers have been undaunted in the face of great hardship.

This persistence reminds me of how the Kamuku team responded at the School of Missions that morning when we received the fateful news about the primary school.

After the 5 a.m. corporate worship of the school, I gathered the Kamuku team to encourage them. "Let us wait for more details about what happened before determining what step to take," I advised.

Unknown to me, however, the Kamuku leaders had heard the news before me, and they had made up their minds to return home immediately. They had only waited for daybreak to inform me of their decision. Their spokesperson said, "Our minds will not concentrate on what is happening here while we don't know what is happening with our people at home." I agreed, and so they returned home.

I was encouraged by their faith before – as you will be when you read the testimonies in the rest of this book. Now, I am inspired by their strong faith that has grown over the years. When tested internally, their faith encouraged me. When tested externally, they stood strong, and their faith amazes me.

What a Kamuku convert named Dila said so many years ago rings even truer today: "Let the persecutors come and do their worst. After all, it is better to die on a higher ground than to die in the valley."

1

WE WANT A ZINC ROOF

For we live by faith, not by sight.
2 Corinthians 5:7 (NIV)

Our mission organisation was named Calvary Ministries, known popularly as CAPRO, and the field leadership asked my wife and me to start a new station. We were specifically asked to find a place across the Ukuru River. The idea, besides spreading the workforce, was to be near a large family whose head had opened the door for the family members to become Christians.

The family was large, so we could not find accommodation in their compound. The rainy season had started, so building our own house was out of the question; the mud and straw bricks could not be formed and dried in the rain. But for my wife and our two little daughters, I wanted to temporarily use a nearby makeshift grass structure left by a family of Fulani herdsmen not long before we arrived. Seeing I was serious and feeling it was not going to be convenient for my family to use the Fulani "house," the head of the family asked two of his children to inquire from a man named Biri if we could use his abandoned compound. The year we arrived in Kamuku, Biri and his younger brother relocated to another settlement.

Fortunately for us, Biri agreed. And so we inherited round huts, some only with walls because their thatched roofs had been removed, likely to cover other houses. Only a few roofs remained. But we settled in gratefully, making ourselves at home.

One night we woke in the darkness to discover we had been invaded by termites. In no time they had attacked our books, clothes, and any soft items in the room.

With time, we put up more buildings and continued using grass to roof them in a bid not to look too different from the people. But we had to spread nylon sheets over each roof to supplement the grasses. Nevertheless, the rains still found ways to enter the room no matter how much grass we layered.

When we started to build, our younger and able-bodied neighbours, including those that became Christians through our ministries, seemed glad to stand by watching us mould mud blocks. But they never refused our invitation to eat.

We got on well with them anyway. We understood one another with time. I visited. They visited too. I ate in their houses. They ate in mine, too.

Before long, a few youngsters believed in the Lord Jesus and grew, and to our amazement and joy, a small local church was born.

As our ministry continued among the people, we needed a name to identify our settlement on the map of the land. We suggested it be named after a prominent person. Two suggestions arose: one was living in the settlement and the other was Biri. The problem with the first name was that our village would be called "Owned by the owner of the drinks". We were not a church of drinking the "drinks". So we and a few of the first converts bequeathed it the name Kangon Biri, *kango* meaning dilapidated place. Even if Biri means *monkey*, we were more comfortable with that than naming the place after the owner of the drinks.

A PLACE FOR THE CHURCH

The church in Kangon Biri began meeting to worship under a "Green Cathedral". Two evergreen mango trees with branches interlocking made a towering canopy that provided cool shade. On any other day, it served as a relaxation spot for the villagers. But on Sundays and teaching days, the believers swept it clean and arranged their wooden logs and woven mats to worship God.

Three months after the new church started under the Green Cathedral, the members felt a need to build a house for the Lord. To get a piece of land, they needed permission from the authorities. The chief in nearby Ukuru was approached. He willingly approved the request and ordered the ward head over the jurisdiction of Kangon Biri to show the "church people" where to build.

It was the policy of CAPRO not to take responsibility for building a worship centre for local believers. This is so that indigenous Christians will learn to own and value what they have laboured to build. When missionaries use their own resources to build a place of worship, in most cases, the local people see it as the "church of the missionaries". Therefore, when the new Kangon Biri believers wanted a worship structure, we made this point clear to them. The church understood that its members were to bear the burden of building their own worship centre from start to finish.

So, the church set out to work. Men, women, and children all devoted themselves to the project. They moulded mud blocks through direct labour. An air of joy, teamwork, and enthusiasm filled the air, perhaps similar to how the builders in the book of Nehemiah rallied to build the walls of Jerusalem. Within a short time, the blocks were ready, and a building was erected. The structure had the capacity to accommodate about 60 people.

The missionary team thought the building would have a thatched roof. But the new local believers thought differently: they wanted a zinc roof.

By March, the rain was about two months away, and there was no money to buy the iron roofing sheets and other materials. Grass was also scarce that year. To complicate matters, bush fires burnt whatever grass remained in the area.

The locals use grass to thatch their homes in something like an annual event. Therefore, this meant that thatching the roofs of their homes would take priority over that of the church building. Consequently, using grass for the church was all the more impossible.

Nevertheless, my team continued to secretly hope that the church would eventually give in to using grass, albeit scarce. We were not rich enough to contribute towards their loftier goal, and even if we were, it was important for them to build their own structure. Some on my team suggested that the church use whatever little money they had to search for and buy bundles of grass anywhere they could be found. But the members resolutely rejected this. The Lord's new church building would have a zinc roof. That was that.

By April, the church had not bought a single nail.

The sky began to rumble and signal the coming of rains.

The locals went about preparing their farms for planting.

The missionaries began to fret. *What if the rain fell on the mud structure? What if the newly built building collapsed?*

But the headaches of the missionaries were not the headaches of the local believers, who remained steadfastly hopeful, making no move whatsoever in relation to the roof. They appeared unbothered that they had built a structure of mud and straw blocks that could easily dissolve back to mud when the rain poured heavily on it.

TRYING TO SAVE FACE

Worldly knowledge, if not handled properly, can hinder faith's growth. It makes one walk more by sight and reason than by faith. Uppermost in the team's mind was how the unbelievers in the village would surely ridicule the church. Should the rains destroy the building, they would be seen as foolish. I began to think about Jesus's story of the man who started building a house but could not complete it for lack of a good plan. *The shame of a collapsed church building will actually come to us, the missionaries,* I reasoned. In fact, some unbelievers had started asking us what would happen to the building now that the rains were beginning.

In an attempt to save our face, I suggested once again that the church use whatever money it had to buy roofing grass. But the believers remained adamant, "We want zinc roof over this building." When nudged about whether they knew that no one was coming from outside to finance the roofing for them, their response was that they knew and did not care.

Then how were they going to get the money to do that with less than ₦2,000 (naira) in the church's treasury? That was not sufficient to buy even a single bundle of zinc! At best it would have bought two packets of roofing nails and a few pounds of assorted nails at that time. The zinc alone would cost about ₦20,000, besides the cost of transportation, wood, nails, and the carpenter's fee. Their response: "God will provide, since we are praying."

In May, the seasonal downpours began drenching the roofless building. One side of the wall began caving in, revealing that it was poorly built. To our dismay, none of the church members seemed bothered, despite the evidence melting in plain sight. They all went about clearing and cleaning their farms to start planting crops. To add insult to injury, some unbelievers kept reminding my team, with apparent concern, of the future state of the building when the rains became heavier. "Will your suffering and effort to build go down like this? What are you going to do about it?"

Clearly, the new believers did not understand the "real" situation, nor did the gathering rains scare them. Rather than agree with the church and believe that "God will provide," I sarcastically remarked out of desperation and resignation, "Let's wait and see. Maybe your faith is greater than mine." None of the elders of the church understood the significance of my statement. Maybe they did not care to.

Truthfully, we missionaries had no idea what to do.

I HAVE BEEN TRYING TO REACH YOU

I had a reason to be in the city of Kaduna that May. While visiting our mission's office there, I learned that a Christian brother had been trying to get across to the missionaries from Kangon Biri mission station.

I traced and located the fellow, a businessman. When I found him, the man was excited. "I have been trying to reach you through your missions office in Kaduna here."

I replied, "Yes, so I hear. That is why I came to find you."

"You know," the brother continued, "I saw the good work you people are doing when I spent two weeks on your field during the short-term mission exposure that I participated in. I was impressed by the efforts of the local believers to build a church. I was so encouraged by their faith. Upon returning to Kaduna, the Lord laid it on my heart to buy the zinc for the church to roof the building. That is why I have been trying to get across to you."

Without hesitation, he excused himself and went into an inner room. He emerged shortly and handed me a bundle of notes. "This is ₦20,000. I have kept it for the church in your mission station, specifically to buy zinc for the roof. I should have bought the zinc myself but, when I considered the cost of transporting it to your field, I realised it was better to give you the money. Maybe you can buy it in Kontagora, the nearest town to you."

To say I was dumbfounded would be an understatement! *What was it that God wanted me to learn? Why did God decide to make me see how he was going to honour the simple faith of the new believers in such a way? Does God delight in being pushed to the wall before he acts?* These and more questions puzzled my mind as I put the money away into my pocket.

After thanking the brother for his generosity, I informed him of how he had allowed God to use him to answer the prayers of the new believers in the Kangon Biri church.

SO THIS PRAYER THING WORKS!

I immediately returned to the station to break the good news to everyone. I explained how the money came about and admitted that it was, indeed, in answer to their prayers of faith. I also confessed before the church my initial doubt about the possibility of having a zinc roof.

The congregation was jubilant. The look on the faces of some members seated before me that day said, "We told you God would provide." The look on the faces of others was that of wonder that said, "So this prayer thing works!"

Though we had no idea what to do, the local believers had an idea. They had been praying from the time they decided they wanted a zinc roof. They were watching if God would allow that building to fall. They were taught that God answers prayers. They believed he was going to answer theirs by providing money to roof with zinc in the place where he was going to be worshipped.

The rain continued as the roofing materials were purchased. The weak part of the building was pulled down and rebuilt. Within three days, it was the only building in the village with a shining roof, sparkling for all to see. The same Lord who had provided the Green Cathedral had now provided a zinc crown.

In fact, if the building had been roofed earlier than it was, who knows what disaster might have befallen the worshippers. Everyone, including those who knew nothing about buildings, could see that the building was indeed poorly built because one part was already caving in even before the rains.

The faith of the believers triumphed and was strengthened, while my team's faith and mine was rebuked and challenged. In addition, the unbelievers who had secretly hoped the building would collapse had their mouths shut! Though we missionaries did not know what to do, the new believers did. They obeyed what they had been taught: pray and have faith. And they watched to see if God would allow the building – *his* building where *he* was to be worshipped – to fall.

REFLECTIONS

This is a story of great faith. Faith is accepting in your heart that impossible circumstances will be possible by knowing and trusting in God who can do all things. Some may call the believers ignorant, but they would be mistaken. Rather, their knowledge was based in spiritual truth.

It would seem that the believers did not match their faith with action. But, in fact, they did. In their own words: "God will provide *since we are praying*." Their faith involved both working and waiting for God to work. When they waited, a zinc roof arrived for the Kangon Biri church; earlier they had to work to form mud blocks and stack them into walls. The Red Sea parted before the Israelites who merely stood by, but it is equally true that the Israelites had to take up their swords to do real battle in Canaan. Five loaves and two fishes multiplied miraculously to feed a crowd, yet people still have to work to grow or buy food in other situations. How do you match your faith with action – whether it is work or praying for God to work?

Question: What inspires you about the steadfast hope and faith of the new believers at Kangon Biri? List situations in your life and ministry where there is no possible solution anywhere on the horizon. How can you intentionally renew your hope and strengthen your faith today?

Read: Proverbs 3:5-6; 2 Corinthians 5:7; Psalm 130:5; Galatians 6:9

I reflect back on the dilapidated collection of huts the community had offered to us as our new home, some of which had no roofs. Soon each one had a roof to protect us from the elements. I think of the towering branches of the mango trees that provided a roof over the new believers as they worshipped each Sunday. And now I think of the zinc roof glittering in the sunshine. Surely the Lord, who calls us into circumstances of apparent scarcity, will also provide abundantly. Jehovah Jireh, your provider, has stores from which he can meet needs, stores that we know nothing about.

Question: What is the "missing roof" you have been asking the Lord to provide over your head or over your family or community? List situations where you feel vulnerable to threatening circumstances that you cannot control, like the torrential rain. How can you take steps of courage today?
Read: Matthew 17:20, 2 Corinthians 9:8, Psalm 24:1; 1 Chronicles 29:12

2

HIS WAYS, NOT OURS

Afterwards the disciples asked Jesus privately,
"Why couldn't we cast out that demon?"
Matthew 17:19

She was born a fine girl. At about seven years old, she had never spoken a word in her life but had laughed far more than anyone could remember. Being mute, all she could do to fill the silence when someone spoke to her was to laugh. Her problem started when she was about two years old. She had seizures, was thrown down, stretched, and foamed at the mouth.

Her father strongly believed in the powers of witch doctors to diagnose and treat sickness. So he took her to one. The diagnosis? She was possessed by the "black old woman", an evil spirit which tied her mouth. To open the mouth and drive out the spirit, the witch doctor said, would require a black goat. The father went in search of one. When he found and brought it home, the goat came with her own problems. It was sick and spread the disease to all the other goats in the compound. They all died. Though a great loss, it seemed this did not matter, for all the family wanted was a cure for the girl. Human life and well-being were more important than having many live goats, they reasoned.

One witch doctor after the other was consulted. Goats, fowl, money, time, and energy were eaten up by these visits. But the girl's state only worsened. The seizures increased in frequency. She remained unable to speak. All she could do was to laugh or smile. Possibly that was the reason she was named Dariya, which means *laughter* in Hausa.

CHRISTIANITY COMES

Christianity came to the family through Dariya's uncle, but her father strongly opposed it. However, there was little or nothing he could do. Her uncle, though younger than her father, had three wives, about 20 children, and held more influence in the extended family and the large compound that they shared. In addition to his wives and children, the uncle had wealth and a successful business selling cows. All Dariya's father could do was to ask his own three children not to join what he thought was madness. As far as he was concerned, his brother and his household had betrayed the ancestors.

Nevertheless, Dariya's father sometimes had kind words for us who went to teach in the compound. He would also crack jokes about Christianity and the superiority of his ancestral worship. At about 60 years old, he joked to whomever attempted to preach to him that he planned to make it to 155 years, for he said, "I will become a Christian after 95 years." In other words, *I will never become a Christian.*

Gradually the impact of the light of Christ in the large compound became evident in the actions of the grown-up children of his younger brother. Dariya's father was impressed, although he would not admit there was anything good in Christianity. He kept ridiculing the Christians. One of his popular clichés was, "I will go where my fathers have gone; even if they are in hellfire, that is where I want to be." He would say this with anger in his voice when provoked by the message of heaven and hell.

I and my team taught the young believers in the compound that God can heal the sick through prayers. These children and their mothers believed in that teaching. One day, they offered to pray for Dariya's release from the "black woman's spirit". The father willingly agreed. "Okay, pray to your *Yesu* (Jesus) if he can make her speak," he said. He didn't believe in Christian prayers, yet he could not help but hope they would work for his daughter.

The believers were encouraged. They invited me and I went with one of the team members to join them in the prayers. Whether I and my colleague really believed the prayers would cast away the evil spirit was something else. We had our secret doubts. But the young believers expected an instant answer. Would the girl speak? They prayed so. They prayed and prayed. Their unbelieving neighbours watched with keen interest to see what would happen.

Nothing dramatic seemed to happen.

The believers asked Dariya to repeat certain names and words. She could not. All she did was smile. I was getting embarrassed because of all the people gathered there to watch. *Would the girl's inability to speak immediately after the prayers strengthen Dariya's father's hostile attitude towards Christianity? Would he not ridicule the Christians all the more?*

My colleague and I felt disappointed. *Why would God not answer the prayers to strengthen the faith of these young believers? Why did he not show his healing power to convince Dariya's father to become a believer?* We expected God to encourage us by confirming his word with signs and wonders, by freeing the poor girl's tongue from demonic oppression instantly.

But God was not bound by our expectations; he does things as he pleases. He had decided not to do anything visible on the spot, even though we and the new believers prayed and expected he could. Nevertheless, God did something, both in the visible and invisible world.

SLOW ANSWERS

A few weeks after that prayer that did not produce any result, or so we thought, Dariya's father sent for us. The message was clear, "Come and pray for my daughter again." She had started speaking, mumbling some words that made sense. He wanted prayers for a complete release of the tongue and from the black woman spirit oppressing the girl.

I went with one other colleague in response to the call. I asked if he would become a Christian seeing what the God of the Christians had started doing for his daughter. He was vehement, "No!" He shook his head as if he was asked to do some abominable thing. However, in the same breath, he pleaded, "Please pray that my daughter will get fully well."

With time, Dariya began to talk more comprehensibly and fluently. She attended the teachings and Christian activities both in the compound and at the church premises. She learned to sing like other children. She began to express herself well. For some time, the seizures continued to come upon Dariya, but less frequently than before the prayers. What was believed to be the black woman spirit looked more and more like epilepsy.

Dariya was not fully healed before I left the field. The church, however, kept praying for her. On several occasions, the elders prayed for her by the laying on of hands. They believed that Dariya would someday get complete release from the epileptic seizures. By the time we left, she was doing everything else other children could do.

SURPRISES

While attention was focused on Dariya, God had been moving all along to do something else in a place we were not looking, with a person we were not paying close attention to. Like Mary in Luke 2:19 who pondered the miracle of Christ's coming to her, Dariya's grandmother, a woman in her 80s or so, pondered in her heart the coming of Jesus into her home. Although she barely understood Hausa, the trade language we used, she took interest in the message of the gospel.

One day, she called one of her older grandchildren and announced to him, "I want to be a Christian." The young man showed her how, and that day she put her faith in the Lord Jesus Christ!

The miracle of this conversion was that it took place in her old age. There seemed to be an unwritten agreement among the older generation of Kamuku people that Christianity was a "children's thing". For a woman of her age to freely decide to follow Christ was a surprise to both the local believers and the unbelievers alike. It is a wonder how God works. The Lord was using Dariya's healing in answer to the Christian prayers to talk to Dariya's grandmother. Additionally, the change in the lives of her older grandchildren translated to more genuine love and care for her. Though the believers had prayed for Dariya's complete deliverance from muteness and epilepsy, God decided to open her mouth and then open the door of her grandmother's heart to his Son Jesus Christ.

Some years after my family left the field, the old mama went to be with her Lord whom she found in her old age. Several years later, Dariya joined the company of the heavenly.

REFLECTIONS

Christ has commanded those who believe in him to pray and expect to receive whatever is asked from God. The answer comes as and when God decides to answer. He answers how he deems best. When we worry that our prayers go unanswered, God is quietly doing something beyond our expectations, but in answer to our prayers all the same.

Who knows if we had not prayed for Dariya whether her process of healing would have ever begun? Our prayers may have served to set some wheels on the right track. They may have torn down a strong spiritual barrier or evicted a demonic presence, and having accomplished this through prayer, a natural process of healing could begin.

An answer delayed is not an answer denied. So often the healing, the provision, the relief, the breakthrough, or the transformation we so desperately pray for emerges as slowly as a night sky shifting from pitch dark to light. In fact, the majority of our prayers are answered over time, not instantly.

In Mark 8, we read a story of Jesus healing a blind man, but the healing was not instant. First, Jesus spits in his eyes and lays hands on him, asking, "What can you see?" The man replies that he can see blurry people "like trees walking around". Jesus lays his hands on him again, and this time his eyes see clearly. Why did Jesus take two times to heal him when he could have healed him instantaneously?

We cannot say what was on Jesus's mind, but I wonder if he was giving his doubting disciples a practical demonstration about their spiritual eyes. Just before this miracle, Jesus had been scolding them saying, "You have eyes – can't you see?" Despite so much personal time with Jesus, the disciples' spiritual eyes were still seeing somewhere between blind and blurry; they did not understand their Master even after some great miracles. Similarly, when an answer does not manifest immediately, some important lesson may be underway that an answer delayed – not denied – will help to accomplish.

So let us never doubt that our prayers, as God's children, are heard in the courts of our Heavenly Father. But let us hold lightly our ideas of precisely how and when they will be answered.

Question: Are there prayers you are praying today for which the answer seems denied?
Read: Isaiah 55:8-9; Mark 8:14-25

To the surprise of everyone, Dariya's grandmother placed her faith in Jesus. This woman was present in the background each time we visited the compound, each time we taught from the Bible. Though she was in the background to us, she was in the foreground to the Holy Spirit.

In Mark 8 mentioned above, Jesus followed the healing of the blind man with a conversation with his disciples. He began with the most important question of all, "Who do people say I am?" Then he asked the more personal question, "Who do you say I am?" This time Peter, after a day of lessons, finally "sees" with his spiritual eyes who Jesus truly is. He answered, "You are the Messiah."

Similarly, after the miracle of Dariya's gradual healing, after her grandchildren began treating her with greater love and care, and after teaching from the Word, Dariya's grandmother announced, "I want to become a Christian!"

Question: Is there anyone in the background of your life whom God may be inviting you to put in the foreground for prayer, friendship, or acts of compassion?
Read: Mark 8:27-29; 1 Peter 3:9

3

DIFFICULT ISSUES IN DISCIPLESHIP

"If you forgive those who sin against you,
your heavenly Father will forgive you."
Matthew 6:14

Monsol must have been impressed by the dramatic change Christ brought into the life of his elder brother who had already become a Christian. To encourage this elder brother and his family to grow in the faith, we sent two student-missionaries on what we called a *field practical* to stay with him. A field practical is where trainees are sent to a church-planting field for one to two months to learn from the missionaries. Upon return to the school, each trainee gives his report in the presence of all the trainers and other students and is then drilled with questions. The field missionary also sends a written report on each trainee.

Their time was fruitful. While they taught Monsol's elder brother's family, they also helped Monsol to understand the gospel better.

Monsol became convinced and persuaded that he needed to follow "this Jesus". However, he had two great hindrances.

The first was that he did not know what his mother would say. In Kamuku culture, children seemed to respect their mothers more than their fathers. If a mother did not buy an idea, the child contradicted her at their own risk. A curse from a mother to a child who goes against her wish was dreaded. We found this fear to be one factor that prevented many young people from embracing Christianity in Kamukuland. If a woman raised her breast skyward and uttered curses to whomever it is that lives in the sky, whatever she said would come to be. Many mothers opposed their children from becoming Christians. Some opposed it for fear of having no one to sacrifice to their family's ancestors.

An incident I encountered brought this clearer to me. Two married men with children had invited an local brother and me to come and "initiate" them into Christianity. We rode several kilometres to their village on bicycles and found the one of the men on his farm.

The first man we met welcomed us joyfully. "Thank God you came," he said. "We have longed to have someone come to lead us to Christianity and to start a church in our village." He then shouted the other man's name. "The Yesu people have come!"

In no time we sat on the grass beside the farm. Koba, my companion, began outlining the way of salvation in their language while I prayed silently that God would convict them to repentance.

One of the men said they were ready to invite Jesus to be their Saviour. Obviously, it was not the first time they had heard the message of salvation. We were about to pray.

"Stop! Stop!" shouted an elderly woman as she ran towards us. She had appeared literally from nowhere. She stopped in front of us and began to scold the two men. "What are you trying to do? You want to join the Yesu people? Who will be giving your fathers food?"

One of the men whispered weakly to me in Hausa, "We are sorry, let's meet another time." That was it. Speaking on behalf of the other man, he told me they would postpone inviting Jesus into their lives because the old woman, the mother of one of them, did not consent.

We left disappointed. Curious, I asked Koba where the fathers of the men were. He laughed and said, "Both men died more than ten years ago." It then dawned on me that the old woman spoke of making sacrifices to the deceased fathers of the men. In her religion, the two dead men still belonged to the family of the living. She knew that Christianity would not allow any form of worship of the dead. The two men were afraid that the old woman would curse them if they acted against her wishes.

So, Monsol's first concern was his mother. His second concern was his wife, who was pregnant with their third child. The pregnancy, they believed, was gotten through the concoction of a witch doctor they had consulted. The doctor's fee was to be paid only after the medicine worked – that is, the woman becomes pregnant, delivers safely, and the child is weaned.

Monsol understood that Christians do not have any business with witch doctors. Now, what would happen if he became a Christian without paying the witch doctor's fee? Would he be allowed to pay when the wife delivered the baby safely, after he had become a Christian? He did not want to wait until she gave birth before becoming a Christian. Could he go and pay the witch doctor now before becoming a Christian? But the witch doctor would not accept it because that would be against the ethics of his practice.

In this dilemma, Monsol approached me for advice. "I want to follow your Jesus, but I have a problem." We discussed the issue, and I asked him to think over it and make the decision himself. My thinking was that if he was to become a Christian, he should be taught from the onset to take responsibility for his actions.

Besides, I was in a dilemma myself as to how to counsel Monsol. The choices available were: Ask Monsol to become a Christian and not to pay the witch doctor. Ask him to delay becoming a Christian until after the delivery of the child and making payment. Or thirdly, ask him to become a Christian now and pay the witch doctor his dues as agreed.

There was a moral question to answer. *Would it be right to ask the inquirer not to pay the witch doctor, since it was an agreement? More so that the agreement was made before the inquirer began to see the light of Christ? On the other hand, would it be right to encourage a genuine seeker to defer the decision to follow Christ on the grounds of an unfulfilled agreement with a demonic agent? If I had preached and taught that Christ came to destroy the works of darkness, why would I encourage paying dues to the powers of darkness before becoming a Christian?* The easiest way out of the dilemma for me, as I thought then, was to throw the ball back to Monsol's court. That is what I did. After laying bare the pros and the cons of the alternatives, I asked him to decide for himself.

Monsol went back home, unsure whether he had been helped or not. Neither was I.

MONSOL'S DECISION

Monsol decided to give his life to Christ. He confessed Christ to be his Saviour and became a believer. Contrary to our expectation, the mother of Monsol and of his elder brother was not much bothered that her sons became Christians, nor did she worry that there would be no one to sacrifice to her late husband. However, she did want him to pay his debt to the witch doctor. He decided to pay the witch doctor's fee.

So, Monsol went to inform the doctor of his new faith and its implications. He was willing to pay the fee before the agreed time. Surprisingly, the witch doctor did not object. He was willing to accept payment before the time, on the condition that the spirits agreed. However, he said he could not consult the spirits that day because it was not the right day to do so.

Monsol returned another day, met the witch doctor, and told him he had come to pay his dues. The witch doctor entered his consultation chamber but returned to tell Monsol that the spirits did not respond to his inquiry; it was not yet time to consult them.

Monsol stood angrily and left with a defying pledge: "I am going. You will not see me on this issue again." True to his word, he never returned to see the witch doctor.

When his mother learned of this, she feared that the witch doctor might decide to get back at Monsol by doing something funny with the pregnancy or the child after delivery. So she took it upon herself to go and pay him.

NEW DILEMMAS

New in the faith, Monsol had other problems to grapple with. Rumours had been around for some time that his wife was having an affair with his neighbour, who was also his cousin. Monsol heard all this but had no proof to confront her. He had attempted several times to confirm from her if the rumours were true, but failed.

Another dilemma was his health, which had seen him going to many other witch doctors and hospitals before he became a Christian. He had a sickness that he believed sometimes made him temporarily impotent. He asked if I would take him out to a good hospital for treatment.

We fixed a date. Monsol sold one of his cows to get enough money for the journey and treatment. On the appointed day, he came over to our mission base. The plan was to go to Bacita town in Kwara State where I knew my doctor friend would give him adequate attention and good treatment. However, I had to change plans without notifying him. I apologized and explained that going on that day would incur some unnecessary expenses. What I said made sense to him, and we fixed a new date.

Monsol left the mission station, but he did not go to his house. Instead, he hatched a plan to discover if there was any truth in the rumours about his wife. He would wait in Ukuru, the town before his village, until late in the night, and then go home. He wondered if his wife, knowing he would be away, had arranged for a "visitor" to come to her. It was late when he reached his home, but he decided to wait even longer under a tree in front of his compound.

Finally, assured that everyone, including his wife, was asleep; he went and gently tapped the door of their bedroom. She opened it, looking shocked to see him.

The fact that she did not ask who was knocking and then her shocked look caused Monsol to exclaim, "So, you have just proven to me that what I have been hearing is true!" She wanted to say something, but he shouted her down. "Now tell me who you opened this door for.

You knew I travelled, so you arranged to meet someone this night. You must tell me who and why at this hour of the night!" He threatened to beat her.

She denied expecting anyone that night. "But you opened the door without asking who was knocking," he insisted. "It must be that you arranged to sleep with another man knowing I had travelled. Tell me who, or I will kill you this night." He threatened her life if she did not tell him whom she was expecting. He also tried to find out if it was true that his own cousin had been sleeping with her.

Then he began to beat her. She cried and shouted for help. Her cries awoke Monsol's elder brother and other neighbours. They came to find out what the matter was. They pleaded with Monsol to stop beating her but to no avail. Monsol had a cutlass in one hand and threatened to use it on anyone who came close, so no one dared to intervene.

Seeing her helplessness, the wife began to confess her past illicit affair with his cousin. It was only then that he stopped beating her. He asked everyone to go back to bed.

WHAT TO DO NEXT?

Confusion began to set into this young Christian's mind. *What would he do now that he had committed himself to be a Christian?* If this incident had happened before then, deciding what to do would have been easy: divorce and remarry.

Consulting with his elder brother who had been a Christian a year or so before him, he was shown Matthew 19:9, where marital unfaithfulness is given as a condition for a Christian to divorce his wife. That was all the encouragement he needed. Monsol decided to divorce his wife.

As for his cousin, Monsol concluded plans to inflict maximum harm on him for sleeping with his wife. But unfortunately for him, the man ran away the morning after Monsol beat his wife. No one knew where he had gone.

While Monsol contemplated divorce, he decided his mother and I must know about it. From me, he wanted to know if his action was going to be Christian. After hearing him narrate the story, I didn't know what to say to him. I could not give him the approval he wanted to divorce his wife. Though she was not yet a Christian, I could not encourage him to divorce her.

He kept on letting me know that it was Jesus himself who said one could divorce his wife because of adultery. All I did was to plead with him to balance the Scripture his brother had given him with other Scriptures that could equally be applied in that situation.

"It is true that Jesus allowed for divorce in your situation," I told him. "But we must learn to take the whole of his teachings into consideration. Jesus also said we must forgive the one that has offended us unconditionally." I went on to open and read to him several passages where Jesus talked about forgiveness, pointing out that while Jesus permits divorce because of adultery, the same Jesus commands all Christians to forgive those who offend them.

Monsol argued and insisted that he must divorce his wife because the Bible permits it. We reached a point where all he wanted was my permission to go ahead and send his wife packing. When I was not forthcoming, it appeared to Monsol that I was encouraging him to disobey a plain Bible teaching.

Although I could not give my blessing on this divorce, I confessed to him, "Monsol, truly I don't know what my reaction would have been were I in your shoes."

At this, Monsol began to shed tears. I was confused. *What did I say wrong that hurt this brother who sought my help? Or was it his helplessness to do what he wanted to do because this Christian thing had tied his hands? Was it the Holy Spirit, convicting him of the wrongness of his desire to divorce his wife?* Later I would learn that it was my admission of not knowing what to do if I were in his situation that made him cry. It softened his heart towards his wife.

A transformation seemed to take place in him after he cried. He returned home in a different frame of mind than he had left with.

FORGIVENESS FLOWS

Though his wife's confession of having an affair with his cousin was a scandal, he arrived home ready to act contrary to everyone's expectation. He called her and reminded her of what he would have done to her if it were not for his new faith, Christianity. He told her he forgave her. Then he encouraged her to consider becoming a Christian too.

All that he told her sounded incredible. This was not the hot-tempered man she had known all the years she had been married to him. When he said he had forgiven her, she found it difficult to believe him. However, she began to see true love she had never experienced from him before. He would discuss and talk freely without shouting at her. Sometimes he helped with the house chores or even took care of the child while she did some work in the house or went to fetch water from the stream. He, too, sometimes fetched water or firewood to the house.

The person Monsol found more difficult to forgive was his cousin. The latter had returned home after some weeks. "Any time I see him, I feel like strangling him to death." Monsol confessed to me, "I truly wish him dead." This feeling continued for about a year. However, Monsol was not happy about it. He wanted to live a true Christian life the way the Bible taught.

One day, Monsol walked alone in the bush looking for locust bean pods, carrying a sharp cutlass in one hand. He came upon a locust bean tree. Lifting his eyes, he discovered more than bean pods. There, high in the tree, was his cousin. The cousin saw him, too.

Many thoughts flashed through Monsol's mind. *Now the moment you have been looking for has come!* Another thought countered, *But you are a Christian.*

Monsol stood still. He stared up at his cousin in the tree. Then he closely examined the cutlass in his hand.

Meanwhile, the much younger cousin was trembling with fear in the tree. Monsol did not know what happened, but he suddenly found himself throwing away the weapon in his hand. He ordered his cousin to come down. The cousin was afraid. Though he saw him throw aside the cutlass, he did not trust Monsol not to harm him. They were alone in the bush. Monsol understood his fears and told him he was not going to harm him.

Still, the cousin refused to come down.

"Well," Monsol said, looking up at his cousin. "If you cannot come down for us to discuss, I want you to listen to me. You know what you have been doing with my wife. You have betrayed me, but I have forgiven you. I hold nothing against you. However, you must repent from your sins and turn to Christ. Your own religion does not change a man from the wickedness in his heart – that is why you could do what you did to me. You know what I would have done to you were it not that I have become a Christian."

Without waiting for a response from his cousin, Monsol left him, speechless and glued to a branch of the tree.

The forgiving heart of Monsol paid off. Not long after he forgave his cousin, he asked for baptism and was baptised. Later, his wife became a believer in Christ, surrendering all her idols to be burnt publicly. She too was baptised. Years later, Monsol's mother, too, gave her life to Christ. The cousin later became a Christian also. Monsol's family and his brother's families became the pillars of the church in Ukuru. His story continues in the next chapter.

REFLECTIONS

There are always thorny issues in a new disciple's life, some of which are brought forward from one's pagan background. In his culture, Monsol was free to divorce his wife. Taking revenge on his cousin was so expected that his cousin ran away. But the Lord allowed Monsol's newfound faith to be tested. Monsol gave in to sin – he beat his wife to the point that even his neighbours begged him to stop. In the heat of his anger, he also could have rushed into the decision to divorce his wife and take revenge, perhaps killing his cousin.

In the case of infidelity, Scripture permits divorce. However, permission is not a command. What is a clear command, however, is to forgive those who wrong us. Every situation of adultery is extremely painful; a hard and fast answer for what to do in every case cannot be provided in this book. But whether the step of divorce is counselled or is taken, the step of forgiveness is commanded.

In the whole of Scripture, we see the astonishing example of a holy God forgiving each of us. His children are commanded to do no less. Even as Jesus Christ hung on the cross dying, he said, "Father, forgive them, for they don't know what they are doing."

Monsol could not have foreseen the eternal impact of his obedience as he was obeying. And neither can we. Our job is simply to obey. Receiving God's forgiveness in his own life and forgiving others changed a man prone to violence into a loving husband. Not only Monsol's wife, but his mother and the cousin who so betrayed him would all one day join him as followers of Christ. Monsol's choice to forgive, and the actions that flowed from it, ushered in a new season in his marriage, his family, and in the church in Ukuru, for the glory of God!

Question: Who are you wrestling to forgive today, whether for some small offence or for a painful, heart-shattering betrayal?
Read: Matthew 6:14; Mark 11:25

As brothers and sisters in Christ, we have the privilege of advising one another. One of the functions of a healthy body of Christ is to provide godly counsel and guidance to one another. Though we may be eager to dole out advice, especially to new Christians who seem to be stumbling about in their new faith, James 3:1 cautions that "we who teach will be judged more strictly". Whether you are a missionary, teacher, church leader, friend, or family member, take on humility when you take on the role of a counsellor.

Prayerfully study the verses and write down any new insights you observe. What kind of counsellor have you been in the past, and what kind of counsellor do you want to become? Commit to prayer any relationship today where you are in the position of an advice-giver.

For the new believer to grow and mature meaningfully in Christ, he or she needs to be allowed to make certain difficult decisions by himself or herself from the outset. In this way, he or she can practise and become someone "who correctly explains the word of truth" (2 Timothy 2:15).

The very best way to guide a new believer to Christian growth and maturity is to appeal to the supreme authority of the Bible over every Christian and as the standard for decision-making. By this the believer knows that whatever he or she decides to do in any given situation is based on the teachings of the Bible, not just a suggestion from humans.

Question: Are you in a role where someone has invited you to speak into a difficult dilemma in their life?
Read: James 3:13-18; John 16:13

4

A PREACHER, NOT A PATIENT

Then he touched their eyes and said,
"Because of your faith, it will happen."
Matthew 9:29

When Monsol became a Christian, people around him knew it was for real. The missionaries and other Christians knew how much he had struggled before making the decision. His people knew he was a man of integrity who kept to his word. If he was determined to do anything, he did it without looking back.

The dramatic change in him was evident to all. Without being told, he surrendered all his charms to us on a Sunday to destroy by breaking or by fire. It did not take him time to forsake certain destructive habits such as smoking and drinking alcohol, habits which others found difficult to quit months and even years after they became Christians. He gave himself to praying as he was taught. Then he committed himself to learning how to read and write in Hausa. In the process, he bought a Hausa Bible. Within five months, he could read the Bible by himself.

The relationship between Monsol and me continued to deepen. Though he lived quite a distance from my family, he visited frequently and we continued to minister together.

However, Monsol had a problem. He suffered from a chronic illness, and he had spent much money on treatment from one hospital to another and in visiting many witch doctors. When he became a Christian, he mentioned it to me. I encouraged him to trust God for healing. We prayed, asking God to heal him. I assured him that he would be healed without going to a hospital again.

A few days later, Monsol came to me and said that he needed to go to the hospital. I was discouraged. *Why, after all the assurance that I had given him?* However, I did not blame him for not having faith. My concern was what impression I must have created in his mind about faith healing. For sure, I believed God heals without the doctors' input. I was categorical that God was going to heal him, and I had told him so. From what he now told me, it looked like the case was getting worse than before we prayed.

In retrospect, I asked myself, *Did God tell me to tell Monsol that he would heal him? Or did I presume God would heal just because we prayed? Did I know for sure it was God's will to heal him at that time?* In any case, I did not want to take any more chances. I directed him to see my colleague in charge of the mission's primary health work. Monsol was given some drugs, but he kept coming for more. It appeared the drugs were not helping.

The next step was to go to a big hospital again, but Monsol told us he had been to all the hospitals we recommended, and they didn't help. He asked if we knew of a better hospital, he would appreciate our assistance in that regard. I knew one and we made plans to visit it.

The day came. I waited for Monsol. We had agreed to leave early in the morning because it was a long journey, and we needed to catch a vehicle to Ilorin in the southwestern part of Nigeria.

I waited and waited. The sun rose up high. Finally, Monsol showed up.

I could not hide my feelings or irritation. "You are late," I said without returning his greetings. He didn't answer me. I observed that he didn't look like someone ready for a long journey. *Had he changed his mind this time around? What had been happening all morning?* I asked if he was ready for the journey.

He was all smiles. "I think that it is no longer necessary for us to make this journey."

I looked at him curiously, irritated and incredulous. "What happened?"

"Because we have prayed," he told me flatly, "I know God will heal me. So, there is no need to waste our time travelling for any treatment."

I didn't know what to make of it – to become angry that he had wasted my time and upset my plans, or to rejoice that the brother now had faith to be healed without going to the hospital. *Could it be the great expense of the journey and treatment that was discouraging him?*

"That is alright, if you think so," I told him indifferently. But on a second thought, I asked what formed his conviction that he would be healed just like that.

"If I have to go out, it will be as a preacher not as a patient," he explained, "I feel God is calling me to go out, like you people who left your places to bring the gospel to us."

I am not sure I was satisfied, but I was surely stunned and moved by the last statement he made.

DREAMS AND CALLINGS

About a year later, Monsol informed me of a dream he had. In the dream, he saw someone asking him to go and help people in a named village he never heard of before. He asked if I knew where this village was. I didn't know. However, I encouraged him to keep praying for God to clearly reveal his plan.

Monsol's call to ministry had similarities to my own. When I started out in missions, I believed God had called me to pioneer a work in Tal. After our training in the School of Missions, I asked to be released to go. But the ministry's policy was that one must go through a mandatory one-year probation period, and they assigned me to Kamuku.

After one year, I approached the leadership, who said that CAPRO was not working in Tal. Instead, I was asked to pray CAPRO into buying my vision to take the work to Tal. I was not happy about this development. After the second year, I attempted again. I was refused again.

So, I settled down to work in Kamuku, consoling myself with the fact that the lives in Kamuku were as precious to God as the lives in Tal that I was struggling to reach. I learned to submit to the organization's leadership. They were not asking me to sin. If their judgement was in error, God would have a way of overruling, but on my part it would be safer to obey than rebel.

While Monsol prayed for clarity, I asked him to continue studying the Bible and get actively involved in ministry in the local church. That year, Monsol and four others were commissioned as elders of the Kangon Biri church.

WHAT THE CHIEF DID

A number of members of the Kangon Biri church travelled a long distance across the Ukuru River. In the rainy season, the women and children found it difficult to cross the water for church service and other activities. The canoe owners charged them higher rates than normal just because they were going to church. Meanwhile, a few Christian Igbo traders lived in Ukuru. So the church began to sense the need to start a local assembly in Ukuru town to cater for the spiritual needs of these and other non-Kamukus. This arrangement would also ensure that Kangon Biri could become purely a Kamuku church. But this concern remained only a matter of prayer as we carried on with the ministry before us.

One day, I was visiting the chief of Ukuru town and met him with his council members. He welcomed me and offered me a seat among them. Ukuru is dominated by Muslims, and the chief also followed that religion.

"Pastor, I want to ask you a question," he said.

"May you live long, chief. I hope all is well?" I replied, amazed that the chief would have a question for me and announce it in the presence of his advisers.

"Yes, all is well," he replied. "For whom are you leaving Ukuru town? One of you came and went on to Maruba; another one came and went to Kaya. Now you have come and settled in Kangon Biri, in the *bush*. I understand you have started a church in Uchindawa. So I ask, who you are leaving the town for?"

All his councillors nodded in agreement. One of them voiced out bluntly what I thought the chief was trying to say diplomatically. "Maybe they don't want our town to develop. See the school they started in Maruba? Very soon, they will be building a hospital there." The other advisers nodded their heads in agreement.

"Sir, you mean we can start a church in Ukuru?" I asked, pretending to be surprised. "But we don't have a place to build our place of worship."

"Did you ask?" he queried.

"No, sir, but we don't mind building one if we can get a piece of land."

The chief immediately appointed one of his village heads, the same man who was asked to show us the Kangon Biri land when we had newly arrived. "Give them as much land as they want!" he ordered.

There and then they deliberated which part of the town to give us. On the same day, we were shown a place near the primary school. Not long after that, the believers from Kangon Biri church began to mould blocks for the building. Sadly, the chief died before the work on the church began. Nevertheless, the new chief gave us all the support we needed, even though some prominent men in the town were not happy.

A year after Monsol became an elder, he and another elder, Garimai, were asked to start the church in Ukuru. The Ukuru church was actually a plant from the Kangon Biri church where we were based.

A lady missionary who had served in Kamukuland earlier visited one day and commented, "Who would have thought a church would come up in Ukuru?" Yes, no one would have thought that would be possible. But with God all things are possible. He uses whoever he wishes to serve his eternal purpose. In this case, he used the late chief of Ukuru to get his church started there.

VISIT TO THE WITCH DOCTOR

Two years passed without Monsol mentioning anything about his illness. He devoted his time to serving the Lord in the new Ukuru church. Though Monsol and I were now in two different local churches, we did, however, go on ministry outings to visit and to preach together. We related in what might be termed a mentoring relationship. In addition, he attended the weekly church leaders training I organised for the leaders of local churches from our different stations, including for other church denominations.

On one of our outings together, we visited a popular witch doctor, a Kambari man named Rajeba, whom I learned was sick. We saw that his leg was swollen. He told us how he sustained the injury that caused the swelling. I requested that we pray for his healing. He readily agreed because I had been preaching to him before. So we prayed and left.

The next day, I returned with Monsol. Rajeba said, "Thank God you came. Pray for my leg again. I was able to sleep well last night."

"What happened?" I asked.

"Your prayers worked. As you can see, my swollen leg is healed."

"Alright, we will pray again. But what are you thinking about this Jesus who is now healing you?"

He laughed. "Oh, you this small boy! You have come with this your *Yesu* again. Will you not let me alone?"

I told him I would not until he comes to Jesus to save him from his evil ways.

"But I have done no wrong," he protested. "My work is to help people with their problems. This is how I get my livelihood. If I become a Christian, what would I eat?" He went on to lecture Monsol and me on the different categories of medicine men and herbalists. He said there are quacks even among them, and some use trickery on their clients, but that (according to him) the genuine ones don't ask for much money for their services. Then, as if his telling us about his work might make us forget his request, he stopped abruptly. "*Mallam*, pray for my leg."

I asked Monsol to pray, but the witch doctor would not have that. He looked at Monsol suspiciously, apparently not sure his prayers would work the way mine did. I told him it was the same if Monsol prayed. God would answer. But Rajeba was adamant.

"Pastor, it is you I want to pray for my leg. This boy is still learning." I was obliged to pray. But while praying, he interrupted. "I want you to put your hand on the leg like you did yesterday." I asked Monsol to join me. The man did not mind the additional hand as long as I was the one pronouncing the words and my hand was touching his leg too.

Funnily enough, while we prayed, the witch doctor was busy talking to a Fulani woman who had come to consult him on her problem. He gave her some powdery substance and described how she would use it when she returned home.

I could not help teasing him. "If you have this powerful medicine that can heal, why didn't you heal yourself?

"Have you ever seen a doctor treating himself?" he chided me calmly.

"Then why didn't you pay attention when we prayed for you?" I asked.

"This boy, just leave me alone. You were doing your thing and I was doing mine." We both laughed. Monsol just watched and smiled.

Monsol and I returned to the mission compound. He expressed surprise at my being free talking anyhow with the witch doctor, whom many people dreaded. He was even more surprised that it was the witch doctor himself who asked us to pray this second time.

GOD'S TIMING

The next time Monsol raised the issue of going out as a missionary, there was a growing interest from other members of the church and from other stations to go out as missionaries too. This became a concern to the missionaries and the ministry at large because those indicating interest to go out of their homeland as missionaries were the very active members of their respective local churches. If they left, those local churches would be weakened. So the missionaries did not encourage them to go out at that time.

It appeared that Monsol was not going to realise his dream of going out as a preacher. However, he continued ministering in the Ukuru church and playing leadership roles in the church and among the believers in the land.

By the time my family and I left Kamuku field, Monsol was growing strong in his faith and zeal for the Lord. My family and I had gone to serve in Tal. I realized then that I would have shipwrecked my faith and ministry in Tal if I had gone immediately after the training, as I wanted to. God wanted to use Kamuku to prepare me for Tal. In retrospect, God's timing was not mine.

Some years later, Monsol called me and said he wanted to go to the School of Missions. So he and his wife trained in the CAPRO Hausa School of Missions for three years. Some years after Monsol and his wife graduated, I became the principal of this school. Thereafter, they started ministry as missionaries.

Interestingly, the name of the place that was given to Monsol in a dream while I was there turned out to be real. He had made inquiries and was able to locate the village. It was to that village that Monsol went to work as a missionary. Indeed, he went out as a preacher and not as a patient. Praise God!

I was once impatient with Monsol being late for our trip to the hospital, but it turned out he had other plans. So, too, both Monsol and I found out that God is not late, if only we can trust his timing and his plans.

REFLECTIONS

When he was considering divorce, Monsol was wise to seek counsel from more mature believers, both from his older brother who had been a Christian longer than he had, and from the missionaries. Proverbs 11:14 describes how "there is safety in having many advisers".

And yet, it is common to receive varying perspectives, even seemingly contrary input, from believers around us. For instance, I gave Monsol different perspectives on how to find healing – first offering prayer, and then offering to take him to the hospital. While this may feel confusing, I believe there can be greater strength and wisdom found in listening to and sifting through diverse perspectives.

However, our ultimate source of counsel is none other than the Holy Spirit, whom Scripture calls a "Wonderful Counsellor". There are times when one must take all the human counsel one receives and go away to seek the face of the Lord alone. Clearing our minds and opening our spiritual ears, the voice of the Holy Spirit can reveal through prayer what to do in our particular situation at a particular time. And then we must determine to obey it.

Question: Are you in a difficult situation today where you do not know what to do? What are you doing to seek godly counsel from believers and to spend time in the Word?
Read: Proverbs 3:5-6; James 1:5; Romans 12:1-2; Proverbs 15:31-33

I felt a call from God to a specific place, Tal. Monsol was called in a dream one night to a named village. But in both of our cases, our leaders at that time did not send us to our place of calling. However, both Monsol and I one day fulfilled these callings, with the leadership's blessing.

In the Old Testament, young David also had a calling from God to be the next king of Israel. And this was not just in his imagination, for the call was confirmed by being anointed by God's own prophet, Samuel. But it took years to be fulfilled, and in the meantime, another king sat on the throne.

One fateful day, David was offered the perfect chance to bring his revealed calling into reality. In 1 Samuel 24, David and his men were hiding deep in a large cave from King Saul and his army. Saul entered to relieve himself – alone and unprotected. Was this amazing situation God "opening the door" to pursue his calling? After all, the years were slipping by while his call remained unfulfilled, and his life as a fugitive hunted in the wilderness was very difficult.

But David did not hear from the Lord to seize the opportunity and kill Saul. David even crept so close to King Saul in the cave that he cut off a corner of Saul's robe, yet he immediately felt guilt-ridden and said, "I shouldn't attack the Lord's anointed one, for the Lord himself has chosen him" (1 Samuel 24:6).

Did the Lord appoint this situation to happen? Yes. Did the Lord do it so that David could finally stride forward into his calling? No. I believe the Lord was testing David's willingness to hear his voice, submit to him, and resist sin though the rewards for sinning would have seemed to some to fulfil God's plan. David proved he could submit both to the Lord and to the current king. Though Saul was sinning in trying to kill David, this did not justify David to kill if the Lord did not command it.

Question: Are there leaders above you today whose position and decisions you are inwardly resenting or outwardly resisting? How can you renew your prayers for them and how can you emulate the attitude of David?

Read: 1 Samuel 24; 1 Peter 5:1-7; 2 Corinthians 6:1-10

5

ARE YOU GOING MAD?

"The seeds that fell among the thorns represent those who hear the message, but all too quickly the message is crowded out by the cares and riches and pleasures of this life. And so they never grow into maturity."
Luke 8:14

From his outward appearance, Jani personified irresponsibility. He had left home many years back. He wandered from place to place such that his relatives did not know his whereabouts. At over 40 years of age, he lived his life drinking and smoking, he was not married, and none of this bothered him.

What could have passed for a house was a round, makeshift structure made of guinea corn stalks topped with a grass thatched roof. A casual observer could mistake it for a farm hut. The only furniture in the room was a bed made of corn stalks with a threadbare plastic mat laid over it. A closer peep into the room showed few signs that a human being lived therein.

He lived from hand to mouth by working on other people's farms. Sometimes, he cut and sold firewood to buy food in the market. You met him at home only when he was sick. His neighbours hardly saw him except to hear his movements when he went out early in the morning and when he returned drunk late at night. He was in rags most of the time. The lifestyle he chose for himself and the way he worked too hard made him look older than he actually was.

All that said, Jani was not a madman nor as completely irresponsible as he appeared to be. He was quite intelligent, full of wit and dry humour. He took life easy, accepting and living each day as it came. He might have looked like a fool, the way he allowed himself to be used as cheap labour by those who took advantage and exploited his simplicity. But you could not take him for granted. He was a man in control of his life.

Jani had a transistor radio set. He was current with the news around the globe. He hardly ever missed tuning in to the British Broadcasting Corporation (BBC) and Voice of America (VOA) news Hausa services. In addition, he listened to programmes in Hausa on the Federal Radio Corporation of Nigeria (FRCN) Kaduna Station. He rarely missed the gospel message programmes on Sundays.

Jani claimed to be a follower of a certain faith other than Christianity. However, he was far from practising. Jani began to show interest in Christianity with the coming of the missionaries to the area where he resided. He had observed their lives and those of the new believers and was impressed by what he saw. He concluded that "Christianity seems to make more sense." However, he thought the type of Christianity he had observed might not mix well with his drinking habits. "Count me out from anything that will stop me from drinking *burukutu* (the local brew)", he had confided in an Igbo trader who had been urging him to become a Christian.

Some time later, he thought he was ready to try Christianity. He wanted to approach any one of us he had seen pass by his house, but he felt shy to do so. One day, he summoned courage and asked the Igbo trader, "How much do I need to pay to be bathed (converted) into Christianity?" He was told he needed to pay nothing to become a Christian.

Although the trader was a professing Christian, he was not sure of how to lead one to Christ. Therefore, he invited me and another missionary to meet with Jani, who had been informed beforehand that we were willing to help "bathe" him to become a Christian.

JANI GETS BATHED

On the appointed day, led by the trader, we went to see Jani. He was not at home when we arrived. He had gone to drink in a nearby compound. We followed him to the compound. There were many people. It was a festive period for another religious group. Some idol worshipers decided to show solidarity with them, feasting and drinking.

Jani was participating in the communal drinking, sharing the drink from the pot with all the men who sat in a semicircle. When he saw his trader-friend with us, he remembered the appointment. He quickly handed over the pot of wine to another fellow. "*Na yi baki* (I have visitors)", he said as he excused himself. He came over to meet the visiting team, full of apologies.

Seeing the state of the man we had come to lead to Christ, we were full of unasked questions such as, *Could someone like this and in this state of mind make a true and intelligent commitment to follow Jesus Christ?* Our natural response was to suggest to the trader to go back until another time. Somehow, we changed our minds. Jani was not drunk after all. More so, going back would signal public rejection of the man we had come to see, and the trader would be disappointed.

So, we stayed and explained the way of salvation to Jani. He said he understood and there made a commitment to follow Christ. The unbelievers looked on curiously. "Is this man deceiving this people or what?" some asked. "He will not last in this new way," some said sympathetically, more for us than towards Jani. Others even predicted, "A dog will go back to its vomit, and a washed pig back to its mud."

It did not take Jani as long to stop drinking as it took him to stop smoking. Nevertheless, that he stopped both seemed incredible to all who knew him. It became a popular saying, "Even Jani has joined the Christians and has stopped drinking." Some remarked, "If Jani can stop drinking and smoking, anyone can."

In the aftermath of his conversion, he began to dress well and his face began to literally shine. His former friends and associates were the first to notice. One day, someone stopped him on the way and remarked, "This

Christianity has done you good. See, your body is looking smoother than before." More people made similar remarks in the hearing of some of us and the local believers saying, "Christianity has 'washed' Jani."

A MAD MAN

Jani admitted that besides having the joy of salvation and peace of mind he got in Christ, he had also become bold enough to stand before many people to speak. He stood before the congregation when he later became the secretary of the church in Kangon Biri. Many people who knew him before agreed that his speech had greatly improved.

Jani began to improve his reading and writing in Hausa. He got himself a Hausa Bible and a hymn book. They became his constant companions, even when he went to farm or hunt. He hardly ever missed Sunday service or any other activity in the church. The long distance from his house to the church never became a hindrance to attending late evening programmes. His zeal, punctuality, and hard work became an encouragement to other believers.

One Christmas Eve, the local church met in the evening to praise and thank God for the salvation that came to humanity. They rejoiced that God made them partakers of his salvation through Christ. While everyone was delighted and jubilantly singing, I decided to test if the church's joyful singing was truly in the spirit of understanding and appreciating the occasion. I asked several questions that were intelligently answered with scriptural bases. Then came the poser – a very ridiculous question:

"Supposing I now, this day, confess to you all that what I have given you is a false religion. That is, Christianity is not the way to God. That Jesus did not come in the flesh, and did not live, die, and resurrect to save us. That Jesus is not the Saviour of the world, that I am sorry to have misled you for these three years or so. Therefore, I am packing and leaving, so that everyone can go back to his former ways. What would be your reaction?"

The church reacted collectively to the question. They burst into laughter as if to say what a silly question. Some voiced their long-time observation of me. "Oh, he has come with his funny but expensive jokes again!"

Jani was not amused in the least. When the laughter subsided, he stood up in the congregation and with all seriousness said, "Well, we will say you came to this land a sane man, and now you are leaving a madman. We can only pray for you."

I had not expected that answer. I was almost moved to tears of joy knowing that I had not laboured in vain among this people after all.

BACK TO HIS VOMIT

A few years after I relocated to another tribe in a different state in Nigeria, it was reported that Jani had backslid in protest of what he thought was an unfair treatment of him by some missionaries.

The real issue remained cloudy to me, even when I visited the field to investigate. The church members had stories to tell about Jani. The missionaries had their own version. Jani felt both the church and the team rejected him. From my findings, it seemed that people from another faith lured him with some material gifts and a promise of a wife if he rejoined them. Their offer appeared irresistible. He began to associate more with people from that faith and began to miss fellowship more frequently. When confronted over the matter, Jani took offense and felt he was being falsely accused. He accused the missionaries and the local church of not caring to know what was happening to him.

Nevertheless, at some point, Jani returned to fellowship. Then he spent about a year with my family in Tal field, Plateau State, Nigeria, where we began a new work after we left Kamuku. Jani continued to be discipled along with the new believers from that field. At the end of his stay, he returned with the promise to continue in the faith. My family gave him some money to start a business to sustain himself. He bought second-hand clothes in the city of Jos to sell.

Sadly, not long after he returned, there came another report that Jani had gone back to his vomit. This time, he did not want to have anything to do with Christians. He was not even willing to see me, his former mentor and missionary friend, though we had spent a year together. When I visited the field, Jani tactically avoided meeting me.

The local church and the team continued to pray and hope for the full restoration of Jani to the faith. To Jani's credit, though he cut off from fellowship, he esteemed the Christian faith highly. In his own words, "I will never say anything bad about Christianity, because I know what it has done for me."

CONVERSION OR COOPERATION

Many questions, however, continued to bother me, having played a key role in Jani's sojourn into the Christian faith. *Why did he go back to his former faith? What went wrong with his conversion and conviction? Was Jani genuinely converted to Christ or not? Was it the way he was led to become a Christian that was wrong? Was he truly discipled? Did we who discipled him do a proper work on him?* And the big one: *Can a person who truly became a Christian leave to become something else? Had he lost his salvation?* Many questions beg for answers that only heaven can provide.

In hindsight, I now admit I made some mistakes in asking people if they wanted to give their lives to Christ each time I presented the gospel. It is not certain if Jani actually understood the gospel and made a true commitment to follow Jesus or not. I now believe and teach that people should be allowed to make the first move in the final decision to be Christians after they fully understand the message of the gospel. This seems to be the practice of Jesus and the apostles. In their time, people felt a need and came to ask, "What shall we do?"

But when we insist on making altar calls or asking people to give their lives by raising their hands and coming forward to be led in the "sinner's prayer," it often doesn't produce the real fruit of repentance.

Even the few who stand as true Christians thereafter must have been genuine seekers before the altar call or whatever shortcuts the preachers have invented to get converts. Often it is the missionaries, evangelists, or preachers that "make" the converts instead of waiting for the Holy Spirit to bring about true conviction and conversion. They are in a hurry to make converts. It is no surprise that such "converts" do not last, but God's converts will always turn out to be true disciples of Christ.

It is now over 10 years since Jani's purported return to his former religion. There are conflicting recent reports of whether Jani is fully back to the Christian faith. Whatever is the case, I ask the reader to join in praying for the Janis of this world who may genuinely encounter Christ but get confused along the way. Let's not give up until Christ is formed in them.

REFLECTIONS

Jani's backsliding raised many questions, including some questions Christians ask to ascertain the genuineness of others' faith. Sometimes our questions carry a sense of judgement when we perceive people are not measuring up to our definition of faith principles and practices. Jesus clearly taught that it is not ours to judge others. We should rest assured that only the Lord knows those who are his. We should therefore use the energy we spend on judging whether others are going to heaven instead on righting our own ways with the Lord.

Which is easier: to judge and criticize another, or to obey? Judging takes no effort. Too often it is done to make ourselves look better. I have heard it said that we judge others by their actions, but we judge ourselves by our motives. For example, if in anger we verbally abuse another person, we judge ourselves lightly; we did not intend to verbally abuse them. But we judge another person who does the same by their action, not their intention.

James 3 warns us about the dangers of the tongue. Later James writes, "Don't speak evil against each other, dear brothers and sisters . . . [Y]our job is to obey the law, not to judge whether it applies to you. God alone, who gave the law, is the Judge. He alone has the power to save or to destroy. So what right do you have to judge your neighbour?" (James 4:11-12).

Even heroes of the faith are recorded in the Bible as having disobeyed, rebelled, and broken God's heart. King David, Moses, Abraham, and the whole nation of Israel had rebellious moments: "We have turned away from you and sinned against you again and again" (Jeremiah 14:7b). Whether someone's initial profession was false, or if they have merely slumped into a time of disobedience and wandering, we cannot know their heart. Therefore, we can leave this in God's hands.

Question: Is there someone whom you have been judging who the Holy Spirit is asking you to release from judgement?
Read: Matthew 7:1-5; Luke 6:37; John 3:17

In the parable of the sower, Jesus says that many people will receive the seed of the gospel and initially show signs of growth, but only some will produce fruit. The devil will take the seed from the hearts of some people, others will wither without roots when they are tested, and others will not mature because they are choked by the thorns of life's worries, riches, and pleasures. While we cannot be sure, thorns may have choked Jani's faith, as some evidence suggests Jani was lured by material gain and distracted by conflicts with missionaries.

Sharing the gospel is not easy in the first place. It can be very discouraging when people do not accept the gospel or they accept it only to later reject it – at least from your perspective. But it is important to remember that we are not the Lord of the harvest; we are only workers in the fields. The Lord has called you into his field to plant the seed, perhaps, or to water it. But it is only God who can make it grow. It is God who started the work in their lives; let us trust that God can finish it.

Question: Have you been discouraged about someone's progress in the faith? How can you surrender them into God's hands?
Read: Luke 8:1-15; 10:1-2; 1 Corinthians 3:5-9; Philippians 1:4-6

6

FOR THIS, HE MUST DIE

> Take no part in the worthless deeds of evil and darkness; instead, expose them. It is shameful even to talk about the things that ungodly people do in secret. But their evil intentions will be exposed when the light shines on them, for the light makes everything visible.
> Ephesians 5:11-14a

The dreaded Magiro cult is practised among some of the tribes of northwestern Nigeria. Only males are initiated into it, and all members swear an oath of secrecy. No one outside the cult – women, children, or foreigners – can know who Magiro is and what the initiates do. Through fear and terror, the cult controls religious, social, and judicial aspects of community life.

There were stories of men just disappearing, never to be seen again. Sometimes young boys who went for initiation into manhood never returned because Magiro "swallowed them up" for their mistakes or because they could not endure the hardship of the initiation processes. At times women were fined for alleged offences and forced to pay with their own goats. The Magiro cult also had outings which terrorised passers-by and created great tension.

In years past, a chief priest in the Magiro cult was a man named Baba Dogo. But he had not always been in the cult. Baba Dogo had been among the first Christians in Kamukuland when American missionary Reverend L. E. Tuller first brought the light of the gospel in the 1920s.

Rev Tuller, in collaboration with the few believers he had then, went about from one Kamuku hill to the other exposing the secrets of the Magiro cult. The elders of the land accused Rev Tuller of exposing their idols and their secrets to women and non-initiates. After many threats and attempts on his life had failed, they reported him to the Native Authority in the town of Minna. He returned the second time and still stirred the hornets' nest. He was deported again.

When Rev Tuller was expelled in 1953, the believers scattered, and Baba fell into the darkness of idolatry, even becoming a chief priest of Magiro.

After some time in the cult, Baba Dogo returned again to Christianity. By that time, the Baptist Church, ECWA, and a few other denominations had evangelized a few towns with accessible roads. Then one day he grew sick and needed an operation. A while later, his wife died. In both instances, he felt the church did not give him the sympathy he had expected. Offended and nursing his wounds, he left and joined yet another religion. Thus, over the course of his life, Baba Dogo had twice been a Christian and had twice backslidden.

THE SEED REVIVES

Calvary Ministries (CAPRO) started work among the Kamukus in 1991. Our focus was the other non-evangelised parts of the land where there was little or no Christian witness. Each missionary would learn directly or indirectly that the first and major obstacle to the hearts of the people was their attachment and devotion to their god Magiro.

But in Baba Dogo's heart, something else was happening. In his very old age, the seed that had been planted in him stirred and revived. Indeed, one day Baba called the missionaries to his home.

So we went to visit him and brought with us one Baba Sata of Maikujeri, a contemporary of Baba Dogo's and a believer from Rev Tuller's work. He had been visiting nearby Maruba, where he was invited to share in the Discipleship Training School (DTS) about how to preach to people who practise African Traditional Religion. The two old men, among the first converts from Rev Tuller's work, had scattered after the deportation of Tuller. While Baba Dogo returned to idolatry, Baba Sata continued strongly in the faith, and God used him to plant churches amidst persecution. At this meeting, they met for the first time in about 50 years. It was a day of great surprise and reunion.

In the presence of Baba Sata, Baba Dogo rededicated his life to Christ. He proclaimed, "I have slept for too long; I now want to wake up from my sleep!" He continued proudly to his people, "I am back to Christ now that I have seen my brothers." From that moment, the news spread.

His "brothers", we missionaries, continued to visit and fellowship with Baba. Sometimes I spent days in his house. With time, the joy of the Lord began to radiate from Baba's face and his unbelieving children and grandchildren took note of it. Some later joined the faith. Baba was greatly encouraged.

But people from other religions, who had thought Baba was with them, were not happy. Some thought to dissuade him, while others took Baba's action as a declaration of war on their gods. From the time of his declaration, the battle lines were drawn.

THE CHRISTMAS CELEBRATION

Christmas was approaching, and we sent out many invitations in Kamukuland. Many came, including non-believers.

Admittedly, most people were not necessarily there to hear about the Light who had come into the world to draw them out of darkness. Christmas was a new thing, and they came to see what the celebration was all about. Others came to partake in the love feast that marked the end of Christmas services in that young church. And still others came to dance and make merry.

But one invitation – the last and latest – was sent to the venerable old local, Baba Dogo. The idea to have him speak at the celebration had come that very morning, less than three hours to the occasion. *Would he accept such an invitation? Would it not look disrespectful to the old man?* The church at Kangon Biri and the missionary team thought it would provide an opportunity for Baba to announce that he was fully back to Christianity, as some still wondered where he actually belonged. *But would he be willing to declare publicly at the church what he had declared only in his home to his guests, especially with the battle lines now drawn?*

Anyway, there was no harm in trying, the church and my team thought. We would apologize to him for the lateness. If he accepted the invitation, the young church would live to cherish this rare opportunity, for Baba Dogo had first begun to follow Jesus Christ long before any member of the church or any members of our missionary team were even born.

He could tell the story of how it came to the land in the 1920s, how it was welcomed, and how its light almost died, up until the recent coming of church denominations such as the United Missionary Church for Africa (UMCA), the Baptist Church, and Evangelical Churches of West Africa (ECWA), and mission agencies such as Calvary Ministries (CAPRO) and Harvesters for Christ. What a morale boost it would be for the new Christ-followers who lived in a context where the elders of the land saw Christianity as a thing for small children. It would deepen the church's roots in the knowledge of its own history, and a man in his 90s speaking of Christianity would challenge more elders of the land to give Christianity serious thought.

Baba expressed his surprise at the late and sudden invitation, but he was prevailed upon to leave his village of Kasuwan Dogo to attend.

The problem now was how to get him to the celebration. Old age had weakened his feet too much to walk, and he also had chronic ulcers on both legs. Someone in the church had a motorcycle. That would do. But the motorcycle refused to cooperate. Its clutch cut. A church member graciously agreed to bring Baba on the back of an available bicycle. Baba humbly agreed to come, though it was not going to be fun along the thorny and shrubby bush path.

Back on the mission compound, believers put their heads together to fix the motorcycle. Not long after the bicycle took off with Baba, the motorcycle was repaired. Soon Baba was transferred to it and had a smoother ride to the church premises, though not without some thorns tearing his feet.

EXPOSED

The celebration began, and finally the time came for Baba to take the stage. He sat down before the small crowd, well composed, and spoke in Kamuku to the delight of everyone. *"An an duwo? Do tu neba? Kata gabjiya?"* he greeted, which means, "Have you woken up? How was the night? How is your tiredness?" After he spoke, the celebrants began to ask questions about his long life of experiences.

Then a very unexpected question came. A woman asked, "Is it true that the god Magiro kills non-initiates who cross its way?"

Silence settled over the congregation. Baba tried to evade a direct answer. But he was cornered. The men tensed up. The unbelievers held their breath. The womenfolk strained to know about this god of men who had terrorised them for ages. Everyone leaned in to hear Baba's next words.

Baba's helplessness was evident. Only he and some believers who were former members of the Magiro cult knew the implications of answering that question truthfully. He had come to encourage the church; could he now confess the truth? What would happen if he said what the men did not expect him to say?

One of his grandchildren in the church reminded him, "You are to speak only the truth, Baba."

Baba was quiet for some moments. Then he muttered some sounds that seemed to say, "Come what may, I will speak out." He must have also offered a silent prayer. He cleared his throat.

"It is not true. Magiro does not kill. Rather, it is men who kill people."

Fire does two things: it scorches, and it gives light. For some, the truth Baba spoke seared them like a fiery dart. For others, the truth was a beam of light, glowing brighter as his words settled in.

And like a fire, the news spread: "Dogo has shamelessly exposed private things before women and children." People exclaimed, "The atrocities attributed to Magiro are actually committed by men!" The women and children who once had rushed for cover during Magiro's outings now said with wonder, "Why, it is just men who go about producing loud sounds with metals and other objects, claiming these to be the cry of the gods."

Over 70 years after the Rev Tuller exposed the secrets of Magiro, history was repeating itself. This time, the centre of the controversy was none other than a convert from Tuller's work, an insider and a native of the land, old in years and well respected.

The truth was out. The acts attributed to Magiro were now known to be perpetrated by mere men who masked themselves as gods. Baba Dogo had not only declared himself a true follower of Christ, he had also declared the falsehoods of the cult and enraged its adherents.

This disclosure was received with mixed feelings. The young believers sighed with relief. Their position in leaving the way of falsehood, the way of the ancestors, was now vindicated by no less of an authority than a former chief priest.

The womenfolk, both Christians and non-Christians, rejoiced. At last, the secret of how men oppressed them was exposed. In fact, some of the women went about telling the men after the service, "We now know your secrets. Baba has told us everything." They had lived in fear and oppression, but now they could resist those who had lied, intimidated, extorted payments, and killed their loved ones.

Believing men who had once been members in the Magiro cult witnessed a former chief priest speaking the truth. They would soon see if the power behind the oaths of secrecy would prove to be deadly, or nothing more than dry leaves tossing helplessly in the wind.

However, the whole thing did not go down well with the unbelieving men in the congregation. "If he were not an old man, I would have struck him dead," one elderly man reported to another after the service.

As the news spread, the elders of the land involved in the Magiro cult whispered among themselves and counselled one another: "Something must be done."

SOMETHING MUST BE DONE

The majority of the elders agreed that the missionaries must be expelled from the land. Then the gods should be invoked to afflict the indigenous believers with a disease that causes the belly to swell. Finally, subject to the ratification of the larger council of elders of the land, two men must die – Baba and me, who had invited him.

These threats of the pagans came up to the hearing of the men in the church. They were taught to expect persecution. They knew that Baba caused a ripple in Kamukuland, and his life was in danger. Therefore, they called for prayer and fasting – for the safety of the old man and courage for Christians, that none would fall back when persecution was unleashed. We encouraged the local believers not to fear, assuring them of God's control of the situation. Some still feared and wondered, *Will this new God save us from Magiro's wrath?*

One new believer did not pretend to be unafraid. "Well, if you see people's stomachs start to swell, know that Magiro has started his work," she announced, looking troubled.

Other believers told her, "Jesus has power over Magiro. If you are a true Christian, can Magiro have power over you?" And so they encouraged themselves and continued to pray.

We also learned that the priests of Magiro would invoke the gods to execute justice against us and planned to achieve this not only through the Magiro of the land, but also the Magiro of the neighboring Kambari tribe. It was widely believed that the Kambari had the most powerful Magiro of the surrounding tribes. Therefore, people were sent to confer with the priests of that tribe, for the Magiro of Kamukuland seemed to have been defied.

While we worried over what would become of Baba, the old man remained calm. He admitted that in earlier times, he would have been killed without notice. Yet his heart remained unshakable. "Since we believe in God, you just go and continue to pray for me. If they say I exposed their secrets, let them come and confront me directly, and I will expose more secrets! When they killed so-and-so, they said it was

Magiro. When they killed the son of so-and-so, they said it was Magiro." One could feel the anger arising in Baba's voice over people's wicked hearts. "Magiro has no business killing people. It is people killing one another under cover of darkness and saying it is Magiro."

Meanwhile the threat to Baba's life and ours continued to gain ground. The elders of the land and representatives of the clans met twice to deliberate over what to do. They met in the bush. Among the elders was a "traitor" who informed Baba what was discussed. Baba, in turn, passed the information to me for prayer.

I contemplated reporting the threats to the district head or to the police. But to my surprise, Baba did not support the idea. He reasoned, "If we report these people, we will win the case, but we will lose the people. They would never want to hear our gospel again."

He felt that some of the rulers of the land or the police might seize the opportunity to extort money from the people, adding to other inconveniences and sufferings they would be made to go through. Thereafter, everyone would hold the Christians responsible for their hardships. "We must continue to pray only," Baba counselled.

Thus it was that the man who once fled in the face of persecution now cared less for his own safety and more for the evangelistic work, the witness of Christians, and the suffering of the people. Though he had defected from the faith twice before, he refused to budge from it again. Though death itself fixed its gaze on him, Baba fixed his gaze on the Light, his fortress and his deliverer.

THE MEETING THAT SEALED OUR FATE

More than 40 men from various parts of the land travelled from far and near for the General Council of the elders of the land. It was the last meeting in which Baba's fate and mine were to be sealed.

The penalty for the type of offence under discussion was death. Normally, no time was wasted in talk. Once the elders pronounced a person guilty, the person died. It remains a mystery, however, why the Council took so long to decide what to do with Baba. Surely God's restraining power – the result of prayers of the Christians – prevailed. Maybe it was also fear of the government, for many people erroneously believed I and my team represented the government. Therefore, they had to take care what they did with these "government agents", as we were called. It was obvious God was at work, fighting on behalf of his servants and his church.

By tradition, the nearest relation of the offender was given the task of executing the sentence, so the elders appointed Baba's nearest kin. "What are you going to do with your 'father'?" the Council asked him.

The man replied, "What has my 'father' done that deserves what you are asking me to do?"

The men looked at one another in disbelief. "What have we been meeting and talking about all these weeks?" they asked each other.

Somebody stood menacingly, sensing betrayal in their midst. "Your father said what should not be said before women and children. For this, he must die!"

The kinsman of Baba straightened up and cleared his throat. "Pardon me, all the elders of our land. I am not refusing to do what the elders and the ancestors have decided should be done. The offence is grave enough. Yet as you all know, in cases like this, the facts about such an offence must come from those who witnessed when the offence was committed. Now what we have been discussing took place in the church. Which of us seated here was present when my father said what is attributed to him?"

The place fell silent. The men began to look at one another in disbelief as if to say, *What type of question is this?*

"It's just like I said!" someone exclaimed. "We are not together in this matter."

Another man shot up. "None of us was there, but we all heard it from the air."

Baba's relation retorted, "That is sheer nonsense."

A second witness stood up. "Well, we were not there, but some of our women were there. They came back to tell us all what the old man had said."

"How interesting," Baba's relation said mockingly. "You all know as well as I that this Council does not take evidence from women. So, what are you talking about?" He clenched his fists and glared.

A third man stood to speak. He was the scribe of one of the local chiefs of the land and appeared learned. "Well," calling attention to himself. "This is not a small matter we are handling. It has reached the big chief in our big town, and he says we must do something concrete about it."

"Where is the letter from your chief?" Baba's relation queried. "Even a chief cannot just send a verbal word."

No letter was produced. No one testified that the accused, being tried in absentia, actually had committed the offense he was accused of. His kinsman, who had a sworn allegiance to Magiro and to protecting his interests, accidentally yet ably defended Baba Dogo without planning to do so.

"So, you condemned a man to death before you proved him guilty? Then I would have killed my father for nothing? I insist that the charge against my father be proven or else I take the whole of this Council to court," the man said with finality.

Grumblings bubbled up like the surface of a pot of stew over hot flame. Surprisingly, most of the delegates agreed with the man who defended Baba. Those who had to travel a long distance began to count their loss. They had left some of their businesses unattended. Those who came by foot talked of how tiring the journey was.

Next came exchanges of hot words, accusations, and counter accusations. The orderly meeting became chaotic. Some suggested letting the matter die down. But the kinsman refused. The least he would agree to was that the most elderly ones among them apologize to Baba. Otherwise, he threatened police or court action. Some felt it was not necessary, while some agreed. Rowdiness threatened to reign again.

With no solution forthcoming, the most elderly among them rose to leave one after the other. Like the accusers in John 8 who dropped their stones and slipped away one by one, the leaders in the meeting also dispersed in different directions. Some left defeated; some disappointed.

Others left vowing to see that the gods and the ancestors be avenged. "Baba must not see the end of the year," they swore.

BABA'S RESPONSE

When all this was reported to Baba, he laughed. "I wish I knew who wants me dead. I would buy salt and distribute it to their wives to show that I have no ill feeling towards anyone." His next words echoed those of Joseph to his brothers who had sold him into slavery in Egypt (Genesis 50:20), "They had planned evil against me, but God brought their plan to naught."

Baba lived for a few more years before he died a natural death at a very ripe age of about 100. We were not expelled from the land, nor did anyone die. None of the believers had swollen stomachs.

REFLECTIONS

Isn't it amazing how God comes to the defence of his people using agents who society may overlook, and even who believers may think unworthy? God can use even his enemies, like Baba Dogo's kinsman. This man, himself a devotee of Magiro, was the executioner appointed by humans, but the liberator appointed by God. God used him to reverse a certain death sentence into a demand for an apology.

God can also use people who have backslidden (like Baba Dogo), women (like the woman who posed the question to Baba Dogo), children (like the Hebrew slave girl who helped her leprous master, Namaan), and even the weather (like the storm that shipwrecked Paul). God can use anyone and anything he chooses, no matter how unlikely, to accomplish his purposes, protect his people, and proclaim his glory.

Question: How can this knowledge increase your faith today in areas where you are facing what seems to be a lack of help?
Read: 1 Corinthians 1:2; John 7:24; Isaiah 55:9

I believe the Lord gave Baba Dogo the opportunity to prove that his turning back was genuine and, indeed, final. Although in the past he had defected from the faith for lesser reasons, the current threat before him was the ultimate one – death itself. Surely, this was a man transformed! Peter the disciple denied Christ three times on the night of Christ's trial, yet he went on to face death and become a "pillar in the church". So Baba Dogo denied Christ twice, but also went on to stand firm in the face of death, and the Lord used him to grow the faith of the fledgling church.

Baba Dogo declared, "Let them come and confront me directly, *and I will expose more secrets.*" Let us be wary of the habit of secret-keeping in our own families, churches, and communities. When you begin to bump into the presence of secrets, consider that these may be footholds of the devil. Secrets must be brought to the light by courageous truth-telling. Surely, nothing is hidden from the Lord.

Question: Are there secrets held in your own life or community that may be concealing sin or injustices?
Read: John 3:20-21; Proverbs 28:13; Psalm 32:5; Hebrews 4:13; Ephesians 5:11-14

7

I'D RATHER DIE ON THE HIGH GROUND

From the ends of the earth I call to you, I call as my heart grows faint; lead me to the rock that is higher than I. For you have been my refuge, a strong tower against the foe. I long to dwell in your tent for ever and take refuge in the shelter of your wings.
Psalm 61:2-4 (NIV)

For a long time, Dila wanted to be a Christian, but her father did not allow her. He wanted all the members of the family to become Christians at the same time. However, this never happened. In her community, family interest overrides the interests of the individuals in the family.

One reason her father and mother did not allow her to be a Christian was because of her eventual marriage. By tradition, a woman should follow her husband's religion, so they wanted to wait and allow her future husband to determine what religion she would follow. Dila hoped she would be given in marriage to a Christian.

But the time came, and the marriage was contracted against her wish. Her husband's name was Mahuga, and he had once contemplated becoming a Christian. The missionaries staying near his house and the local believers preached to him on many occasions. Many times, he had gone up to the point of making a decision to follow Christ, but for one reason or the other, he never made it. He felt unable to forsake some unhealthy habits that he knew Christianity did not encourage.

Finding herself in this marriage, Dila did everything to frustrate and to make sure it did not work. Either they quarrelled and fought, or she ran back to her parents on flimsy excuses. People close to them were fed up. Her parents warned that she should never run back to their house when there was a misunderstanding between her and her husband. Friends and relations got tired of settling their quarrels or going to pacify her. For the first year of the marriage, no peace lived in their home. Throughout this period, she never spent up to two weeks consecutively with her husband, and she never allowed him touch her in bed.

Mahuga was frustrated but desperate. He wanted the marriage to succeed. This was his second marriage in less than two years. The first lasted only three months, and then his young wife ran away. If this one also failed so soon, people would think he was the problem. He had loved the first girl, and he loved this one too. So, to save his face, he bore her excesses.

He went in search of a solution from witch doctors and religious spiritualists.[2] They sold him one charm and the other. But all these failed to keep Dila in his house.

Thinking that being near her parents might be contributing to her misbehaviour, he contemplated leaving the village. He acquired some farmland outside their tribal land and began to make plans to move there with her.

One day he came across Dila's relations who had settled there too. They belonged to a different religion. If he would join it too, they promised to intervene in his marriage. He converted from his traditional religion without consulting Dila. That decision made things worse. She saw her chances of becoming a Christian slipping further away. When

2 Like witch doctors, religious spiritualists offer spiritual means to achieve an outcome such as health or prosperity, or to influence or harm others, but they have greater affiliation with a religion.

he suggested that she join him in that religion, she adamantly refused. She also refused to move to the new farmland he had acquired. Thus, he shelved the plan to migrate.

DESIRE FULFILLED

Time passed and one day, Mahuga told a local church member that he was finally persuaded to become a Christian. Maybe it was to keep Dila from divorcing him. Maybe it was genuine conviction. Maybe it was because someone had earlier encouraged him that if both of them became Christians, their marriage could be built on a biblical foundation and become healthy. He also confided that his new religion had not made any change in his life. But he wanted a change. He wanted a stable family.

For whatever reason, he announced to Dila one day that he was ready to become a Christian. Her joy was complete! She went about telling all who cared to listen. They wanted to make it public by announcing it in the church.

But when the day came, he backed out. He did not attend the service. Dila was disappointed. She could not choose independently of him, because in her culture, that would be interpreted to mean she was becoming the head of the house. If he followed her later, people would mock him saying that his wife dragged him to Christianity.

Nobody knew what they discussed. But the next Sunday, both arrived at church. As was the tradition of the local church in Kangon Biri, those who wanted to accept Christ would stand up to declare publicly their intention, after which they were led to Christ and prayed for by the church.

From her declaration and the way she answered the preliminary questions from the pastor, everyone could see she was sincere and knew what she wanted. The couple were Christians at last. Dila was happy that her long desire since childhood had now become reality.

The quarrels and the fights continued, but not frequently. She no longer ran to her parents' house. People knew little about what happened between them, but the neighbours noticed a change. Their relationship improved. Mahuga confessed later that his marriage was better and that he was enjoying his wife. Both submitted themselves to discipleship. Dila learned faster than Mahuga. You could see that she was really growing.

RUMOURS IN THE AIR

Then one day, rumours began to spread among the Kamuku people that a particular religion was plotting to take over the country and force everyone to join. A few people began to cash in on the ignorance and illiteracy among some people living in remote villages to instil fear. Reportedly, those who refused to join the religion would be killed.

It took us quite some effort to dispel such rumours and allay the new believers' fears. Isaiah 8:12-13 assures us, "Don't call everything a conspiracy, as they do, and don't live in dread of what frightens them. Make the Lord of Heaven's Armies holy in your life. He is the one you should fear."

As for persecution or getting killed for the sake of Christ, we never ceased to teach that these were inevitable. Christians will always be persecuted. On one occasion, I told some of the believers to prepare their hearts for the coming persecution towards Christians generally.

Dila had only been a Christian for three months. Someone put the question to her, "Are you afraid to die for your faith?"

She answered, "No! Let the persecutors come and do their worst. After all, it is better to die on a higher ground than to die in the valley."

Whoever taught her that those who die in Christ actually die on a higher ground and have nothing to lose? Who could have inspired her to speak that great confession of faith if not the Holy Spirit?

THE STORY GOES ON

Many years after leaving Kamukuland, I was introduced during a farewell event organised by CAPRO (Calvary Ministries) for its set of outgoing leaders at the end of their tenure, in Jos. Immediately after the closing prayers, a girl hurried to meet me. "Good evening, uncle," she greeted cheerfully. She spoke good English.

Had I met the young girl before? Her name didn't register in my mind.

"I am from Kamuku field," she said, and mentioned the church she came from. It dawned on me. She was Dila and Mahuga's daughter!

"But you were not born when we left Kamuku. How did you recognize me?" I asked, lost in wonder.

"My mother has been telling us about you." The girl had heard my name called out in the meeting, observed my face when I went up to be prayed for, and took note of where I sat.

"God, you are wonderful!" I prayed.

Mahuga and Dila are still living happily and enjoying their marriage with their children. For almost two decades, they have been standing and growing in the faith.

REFLECTIONS

Dila was desperately thirsty for salvation, but for a long time, her father and her husband blocked her path. She persevered in her search anyway. She knew that in Christ she had found a great treasure, a valuable pearl, and that if it cost her everything, it was worth it. So when the threat of persecution loomed, Dila was unwavering in holding on to her faith.

Persecution is both real and inevitable for the true believer. Choosing to follow the way of Jesus Christ will aggravate and even anger those who are still outside the faith. Jesus and all of his disciples faced trials, hardships, and suffering. In the context of the story, the black cloud looming over the community of believers was the threat of either being forced to join a religion they neither liked nor wanted, or facing death, the highest price to pay for one's faith. Yet Dila, still a young woman and even younger in Christianity, demonstrated the Holy Spirit's new life within her when she exclaimed, "It is better to die for Christ (higher ground) than to die outside Christ (lower ground)." She had counted the cost, and it was worth it to persevere and receive the crown of life.

Question: What is your salvation worth to you? What would you be willing to give up to keep it?
Read: Matthew 13:44-46; 16:24-27; James 1:2-4, 12

In Scripture, we sometimes see someone very new in their faith burst out with a statement that clearly came directly from the Holy Spirit. A Canaanite woman persistently requested Jesus to heal her daughter. A Roman centurion believed that just as his soldiers obeyed his commands, Jesus could say the word and heal his servant. Jesus was amazed at their faith-filled responses, just as I was amazed at Dila's statement. In fact, the only times in Scripture that Jesus is described as "marvelling" is in response to someone's great faith.

Similarly, isn't it wonderful that our exclamations of faith can cause our Lord and Saviour to marvel? These do not come because of our own intelligence or insight, but because of the presence of the Holy Spirit in us.

Question: How can you invite the Holy Spirit to indwell you so that in the face of various threats or needs, the Spirit cannot help but burst out in faith-filled statements that marvel and bless the Lord?
Read: Matthew 15:27-28; Luke 7:6-10; Matthew 16:13-16

8

LIKE MAGIC, THE BEES DISAPPEARED

You faithfully answer our prayers with awesome deeds,
O God our saviour . . . Those who live at the ends of the
earth stand in awe of your wonders.
Psalm 65:5a, 8a

The Kamuku people were farmers. Their primary crop was guinea corn, which was eaten as well as fermented to make the local brew, *burukutu*. The stalks were also used for animal feed or bound together for fencing or to frame roofs. The yearly activities of the community followed the cycle of the seasons: planting, growing, and harvesting; rainy season and dry season. These also marked times for socialising and feasts.

Occasionally, the head of a Kamuku family who had a large farm would call a *gayya*, a day of communal farm work. A great deal of work was accomplished as 20 or 30 men converged on one farm. It was also time to socialize. The older men taught the young men some of the cultural values to do with farming. The one who called the *gayya* would feed the workers during the day on the farm and again in the evening when all those who participated would sit together to drink, dance, and rest from the day's hard labour.

Normally in the evening after the *gayya*, the younger men were supposed to share out the *burukutu* from the big, narrow-necked pot. But that evening, most of the young men were nowhere to be found.

Godo, a man who loved his drink, felt annoyed. It meant that he and a few of his peers had to do the job, for they were the next set of young men. The younger men were no longer interested in drinking and dancing, for they had become Christians and were attending the prayer and Bible teaching that evening under our Green Cathedral. Even the younger ones who were not yet Christians had been attracted to the church by the new songs. So it was that only the elderly people of the village and the likes of Godo were left alone at the drinking place.

Godo was among those who enforced order in the community, both on the farm and during feasts. He saw an opportunity to show his dislike for the Christians. When the songs at the church were in full swing, he came charging. "All who worked on the farm today go immediately to where others are drinking!" he ordered, adding that it did not matter if they had become Christians or not.

His elder brother was a Christian in the church. He and other men wanted to counter Godo's rude interruption with force, but I restrained them. Godo ranted on, stoking a fire that was not lit. He accused me of drawing away their people from their way of life. No one answered him. I explained that nobody was forced to attend the prayer meeting. He had come ready to fight whoever opposed him. But nobody did. He turned and disappeared, defeated.

READY TO CHANGE?

Over the next two years, Godo became friendlier with the Christians and my family in particular. Then Godo's brother, the treasurer of the church, fell from grace. His first marriage had been a failure. After having a child, the woman just left him to live an independent life in the town. After staying alone for a long time, he wanted to remarry. One Christian woman he pursued in marriage turned out to have been promised to someone else since her childhood. Later, another woman he wanted to marry had parents who were not Christians. They insisted that the marriage must be contracted at Magiro's shrine. He agreed. After that, the wife told him that they must convert to another religion. Sadly, he agreed. Godo was disgusted with his brother's decision and accused him of living a double standard.

Despite being more friendly with Christians, whenever Godo was presented with the message of salvation, he would say, "It is good to be a Christian, but it is not yet time for me. When God wants me to be a Christian, I will not waste time. Besides, I want to be a true Christian and not a hypocrite like my brother and some of the people in the church I see. If I want to do a thing, I do it well and not in a half-hearted manner."

Almost three years after my family had been around, Godo finally yielded to Christ, confessed his sin, and became a believer.

Despite Godo's boast of doing things wholeheartedly, we saw little difference in his life after his conversion. The only visible change in his life was that he became gentler. He went about living almost like before. In fact, he was more shameless. Before claiming to have accepted Christ, he would not drink or smoke in my presence. After he became a Christian, he smoked and drank without reservations. He was also slow to learn the basic teachings of Christianity.

Many people inside and outside the church began to doubt if he had genuinely repented. Godo, however, insisted his life had changed for good. He said, "I no longer walk with charms or amulets. I do not seek to hurt people or try to get charms to harm them as I used to do."

On the evening long before when Godo had charged our evening prayer time, he had accused me of drawing his people away from their way of life. I had not answered him then; he had been in a rage. But if he meant drawing them away from their terror of spirits, their curses, and their charms, then yes, I had declared that I did this. Now Godo himself, under no pressure, forsook these things for a higher power.

Godo said he most admired the power of prayer in Christianity. He said it was more effective than any *juju* he had ever used, "Since I became a Christian and learned how to pray, I have enjoyed my life. Nothing seems to go well with me any time I do not pray before going out in a day."

THREAT IN THE FIELD

The rains were approaching. People were busy preparing their fields for the planting season. Godo had gone out to the field early one fateful morning and had forgotten to pray.

He was expanding his farm, so he went about felling trees and clearing bushes. He reached a certain tree. There in its trunk was a large swarm of bees. From the look of things, they had come to settle. Godo knew he could not cut that tree with those bees humming in the trunk. Their settling there meant they would make life difficult for him. They would hinder his free movement on the farm.

He began to fear what he would do. To touch them in any way would provoke their trouble. Their presence signalled the end of working there; he would lose this field until the bees decided to leave on their own. And that may not be for another year or so, when they could find another suitable place for making their honey.

Like all agriculturalists, the Kamuku people lived with the vulnerability that their crops could be destroyed by drought, pests, violent storms, or fires. As practitioners of African Traditional Religion generally, their worldview allowed that calamities could be caused by a curse or by the anger of some god. They also believed specific animals were good omens about the future or life, while others may foreshadow ill fortune, death, or illness. For some groups in Nigeria, an owl hanging about one's property represented evil. People feared a black cat entering a home might be a witch in animal form. Nothing in the worldview of African Traditional Religion was merely what was seen; behind the physical, there always lurked an invisible and capricious world of spirits.

All of this turned in his mind when he remembered that he did not pray before he left that morning. So right there, he knelt to pray, asking God to help him by sending the bees away.

When he finished and opened his eyes, the whole swarm had disappeared! It was unbelievable. In fact, it was scary. But it was true. The bees were not there.

What happened? He could not explain it, so fear began to set in. *If the bees had flown away, at least I would have heard their sound while I prayed. But they just vanished.* He could not explain it. That was the end of the work for the day. He returned home, afraid that God answered his prayers.

Several days later Godo and I were discussing the importance of prayer in the life of a Christian. He narrated his experience to me, and now it was my turn to be surprised, including some elements of disbelief. But Godo insisted it was true, saying he, too, would not have believed if someone else had told him the story. "When I opened my eyes, like magic, the bees had disappeared."

Indeed, what seemed "like magic" in his old worldview was actually the power of God acting on his behalf in response to his prayer. Though evidence of his conversion was not good enough for some people, he had truly converted. He had forsaken his faith in charms and amulets for faith in the power of God through prayer. And God honoured this, though he was surprised and afraid when God did.

REFLECTIONS

When one is raised to believe instinctively that everything in the physical realm could carry ominous meaning in the spirit realm, then one is always on high alert. Godo had seen magic practised to achieve diabolical ends, so seeing such a dramatic answer to his prayer made him afraid.

It can take time for a new believer to get used to experiencing God's mighty power. It can also take time to get used to the loving-kindness and attentiveness of God, especially in a world where gifts often come with strings attached. Have you ever given someone a good gift, and you saw fear in their response? What you thought would bring joy, gratitude, or relief instead caused them to furrow their brow in worry. What might be the hidden fears of someone who receives great generosity, kindness, or power applied on their behalf? The Lord loves to give good gifts to his children, to remind them of his watchful care over them and of his great power that is at work in and for them.

In Luke 5, Jesus miraculously blessed the fisherman with so many fish that their nets began to break! But Peter was so full of fear that he wanted this Jesus to leave. What if this power turned against him? He knew he was sinful. In a boat overflowing with blessings, seeing divine power released on his behalf, Peter struggled to trust that the power was good and not an evil omen.

Question: Have you ever been fear-filled in a boat of blessing? Consider carefully what lies behind your fear, and how the Lord's command, "Do not fear", can comfort you today.

Read: Luke 5:1-11; Habakkuk 3:2

Godo charging into the time of prayer and Bible teaching at the new church was not unlike the swarm of bees in the new field. Both threatened an expanding work – one a farmer's field, the other a mission field. Godo hoped that his swarm of accusations and demands against the Christians would intimidate and set back the mission work. But the Lord of the Harvest planned otherwise.

Threats are inevitable when the kingdom of God is expanding in the world. Some of these threats will come from the old ways of doing things that are harmful to us or displeasing to God. Whenever possible, a threat should be met calmly, by speaking peace. Proverbs 15:1 says that "a gentle answer deflects anger". Jesus himself did not feel obliged to take the bait every time he was accused. He was skilful at diffusing tensions. Other times we must meet threats with power, like when Jesus defied the Pharisees or commanded an evil spirit to leave. He acted forcefully to bring freedom to the oppressed.

Speaking peace or speaking with power may seem like opposite responses, yet both arise from our identity and responsibilities as children of God. Both signal our authority. The knowledge of which one to bring to a situation comes through prayer and spiritual maturity.

Question: What is the "swarm of accusations" that has come up to threaten your spiritual growth or the growth in your Christian community and ministry? How are you being called to speak peace or speak power today?

Read: Matthew 26:51-55; Romans 16:20

9

IT IS GOOD JESUS CAME FOR KOBA

For the word of God is alive and powerful. It is sharper than the sharpest two-edged sword, cutting between soul and spirit, between joint and marrow. It exposes our innermost thoughts and desires.
Hebrews 4:12

Koba was taken out of their settlement when he was a child to attend a primary school in a nearby town. There he saw Christians at a distance. They never meant anything to him. He spent six years in the primary school. When he was to go on to a secondary school, his father, Babu, went and bribed the teachers so that Koba could return home. Babu wanted him back to take care of his many cows and help him work on the farm to feed his ever-growing family of three wives and very many children.

It seemed Koba's six-year stay in the primary school was a wasted one. When he came back, he could not recite the English alphabet all the way through, neither did he know how to write his name well. Nevertheless, if not for his father's intervention, he would have gained admission into secondary school.

Koba grew up into a young man, very hotheaded and always demanding to have his way. Soon everyone was fed up with Koba at home. His stubbornness and quarrelling made even their neighbours desert him. He had few friends, as most of his peers were afraid to walk with him. He was such a person that when he fought, he was never satisfied until he inflicted a wound on his opponent.

Koba also lived a life of lies. According to his stepbrother, "If Koba said he was going somewhere in the east, start looking for him in the west. If he said he wanted to see a man, he would be somewhere with another man's wife."

Koba was a womaniser, but not an ordinary one; most of the women he went after were married. He, therefore, fortified himself with charms and love potions meant to make any woman he wanted fall in love with him. Much of the money he acquired went to consulting witch doctors.

When CAPRO missionaries arrived in the land, Koba and his father were just then having serious misunderstandings. The misunderstanding was between Koba's mother, Araba, the second wife, and his father, Babu. Koba sided with his mother, and the father was not happy. But from Koba's view, his father forced him to take sides – not because he wanted to defend his mother, but because he was fighting his father for himself. Babu, a cheerful and jovial man outside the house, was a no-nonsense man in the home. Koba explained, "He would abuse her, and her children, and I was not ready to take that."

When the tension between Koba and his father grew too much, Koba planned to leave home. He would tell no one where he was going, and he had no intention of returning. One option he turned in his mind was to go and hire himself out to one of the cattle Fulani men as a herdsman. Another was to aim at nowhere until he reached a big town somewhere. There he would hide and find what to do next. He fixed a date to execute his plan.

AN INTERRUPTION

Meanwhile, Babu had shown interest in Christianity for some time. When CAPRO missionaries came to the area, he was among the first people to come close to them. He never committed to follow Christ; nevertheless, he would ride his bicycle for many kilometres Sunday after Sunday to attend church meetings in Maruba.

He was a rich and influential man by the standards of the community. He was a businessman, buying and selling cows. On his business trips, he met with many people of different religious persuasions. He had come under much pressure from his business associates from another faith to become one of them. But he resisted. He had some admiration for Christians and their way of life. Now with the missionaries around, his attraction grew stronger. He was particularly impressed when they began to render acts of charity, such as taking sick people to the hospital without charging them money. He began to compare Christianity with other religions.

One day, Babu invited my colleagues and me from Maruba station to come speak to his family about Jesus. At times, families would invite us to come and preach to them, and we seized those opportunities the best we could. This invitation through its head was one of those I and my team willingly accepted. However, he had not informed his household.

Koba had made other plans for that week. He was leaving home.

We arrived at Babu's compound and met quite a number of people. Babu was there to welcome us. After a show of traditional hospitality of offering water and mats for us to sit on, he summoned everyone in the compound. There were over 30 people.

"Come and hear about *Yesu,*" he announced. We began to teach them about Jesus. It was not certain if the audience, which included some men who came from other villages to drink, actually understood the message. Nevertheless, interest was keen. The children were excited; they wanted to hear more stories.

While we were preaching, a new idea formed in Koba's head. He had learned that these preachers also teach people how to read and write. He reasoned, *Maybe I should stay and learn from them how to read and write before leaving home, so that wherever I go, I will easily find my way.* And thus he decided to delay his escape. But after six years in primary school without learning the alphabet or even to write his own name well, how could such a scheme work?

CONFUSED CONVERSION

It took more visits before Babu informed us that his family was ready to embrace Christianity. We arrived on the appointed day, encouraged. But after we had preached and explained the implication of becoming Christians, Babu was no longer sure if he personally wanted to make the commitment that day. Nevertheless, he urged us to go ahead to convert his family.

In such a situation where the husband is not ready, the first wife is the one to first accept Christ. However, Mewau insisted that unless her husband submitted first, she would not. The other two wives reasoned the same way and refused to be led in the sinner's prayer.

Then the eldest son was urged to start. He also refused, saying since his parents did not want to, he, too, would not. Besides, he argued that it was his father who invited the people.

After much explanation and teaching, Babu finally agreed to be the first to convert in the family. He was led to Christ, and then the rest of the family were willing to follow suit. In truth, some did it out of duty and loyalty to please the head. Koba, of course, saw it as a way of learning how to read and write. Yet, there were those who agreed to convert because they truly understood the gospel and were under conviction to follow Christ.

How would the preachers know who was real and who was not? Even if they knew, would they have cared if everyone professed Christ by repeating after the preachers the sinner's prayers? This was the first family in that part of the land to embrace Christianity. There would be the joy of reporting such a mass conversion to the outside world. Therefore, we were very eager to lead all the members of the families to Christ, except the younger of the children who didn't understand Hausa and could not repeat the prayer of repentance after us.

A STUDENT AGAIN

The day we asked the members of his family if anyone wanted to accept Christ, Koba said "yes". Much later he would confess to me, "In my mind I knew that I didn't want to be a Christian. All I wanted was to learn how to read and write."

He committed himself to learning how to read and write to the point of irritating me. When I went to teach basic Christian doctrines in their compound, Koba would not pay close attention. But as soon as this was over, he was beside me with one question or the other. He would want to write the alphabet for me to see if it was correct, or to recite the alphabet to hear if he said it well. I paid him attention anyway. This paid off. Within a few months, Koba was reading Hausa reasonably well, to the surprise of many people in his community.

Somehow, the Bible teachings began to make sense to Koba. But they didn't mean much to him. However, in order not to lose his chances of learning more from me, he reduced the rate of his fighting and quarrelling with people in the compound. He feared if he was reported, I might stop teaching him.

Later he would say, "Whenever I was alone, I would speak badly about Christians and their God so that the 'spirit' would not catch me and make me a Christian." On one such occasion, one of his younger siblings overheard and confronted him.

Koba would also get annoyed if his stepbrother took a long time praying over the food. He detested anything Christian, yet he pretended he was one.

He had read over and over the few elementary books he was given. He had nothing else to read. The only advanced book he could find was the Holy Bible in Hausa. So, he borrowed it from one of the missionaries and started reading from Genesis.

Because of his zeal and commitment to reading the Bible, everyone thought he was a zealous Christian. But Koba, and maybe others in his family, knew he was not. His mother, Araba, mocked him. "If all Christianity is like Koba's, nobody would be a Christian."

KOBA READS THE WORD

As he read book after book of the Bible, he began to admire it. He was fascinated in particular by the practical life advice the book of Proverbs offered. He read the book of Proverbs twice and saw that it had much to tell him about his life. He saw where his life was heading and the consequences of his plan to leave home. He saw how the relationship between a wise son and his parents should look. He was overwhelmed and convicted of his heart's true state.

One day, Koba went into the bush alone. He cried and asked God for forgiveness. He stayed for a long time, crying. Then he asked the Lord to come into his life. From then, he said, "I decided to read the Bible more to know more about God and what he had to say to me."

Koba's younger siblings were the first to notice the real change that came over him. He no longer cursed, abused, or bullied them as he used to. Suddenly, Koba, who used to be talkative, became a reserved person, talking only when he was spoken to or when necessary. I observed this change and was moved to ask him why this change, thinking perhaps there were some issues in the family again.

"Nothing," he said. "I am trying to adjust to the demands of the new faith. I have become quiet so that I will not be telling lies again. I read from the Proverbs that those who talk too much often tell lies." By this, he was referring to his days of being a womaniser. As for womanising, he continued in secret for about a year until the Spirit of God "caught" him. And when God did, he yielded. His transformation was visible.

His father and mother, though not stable in the faith, were very happy. The mother could not hide her happiness. One day, she was pondering on the purpose of Jesus Christ coming into the world. Then she turned to someone in the compound, "I don't fully understand this thing about Jesus coming to die for the people of the world. They keep on saying that Jesus came to change the people of the world. Even if he didn't come for the people of the world, it was good he came for Koba. He has changed him for good."

Koba has grown up to become an elder and a teacher of the Bible in his local church. He is also involved in community development and completed a course that prepared him for this. He later joined the Indigenous Church Planting Team to continue the church-planting work in Kamukuland where the missionaries stopped. Koba and his wife now work in another part of the land as missionaries.

REFLECTIONS

Many people in Kamukuland came to us with motivations different than our missionary team would have preferred. Some wanted healing, many wanted freedom from the terror and oppression of evil spirits, some wanted to eat at the Christian feasts or enjoy music, others were driven by curiosity. Of course, we did not criticise or accuse anyone for these motivations.

Although Koba's desire was to succeed in his goal of running far from home, this desire served to put him in a place where he would be friendly with Christians and hear the Word. His motive was literacy; his method was false conversion; but the outcome set by the Lord prevailed – his salvation.

Hebrews 4:12 describes the Word as "alive and powerful. It is sharper than the sharpest two-edged sword". This is a dangerous weapon to manoeuvre; it is not a tool one can casually pick up and play with. Koba could not use it merely to practise reading; it began to cut to his heart, penetrate his mind, and expose his innermost self.

If you know people who are interested in Christianity, who ask you for prayer, or who are curious about the Bible, don't worry too much about their motivations. Allow them to experience God's power and to hear his truth, and trust the Holy Spirit to do the rest.

Question: Do you know people who appear curious or open to learning more about Christianity for whatever reason? How could you invite them to experience God for themselves?
Read: Hebrews 4:12; John 6:44; John 15:16a

Koba's agitation and irritations about Christianity are not uncommon for many people in the season before they surrender their lives to Christ. In Kamukuland, we regularly received verbal attacks, mocking, and other hostile actions, often from people who would one day put their faith in Christ and join the church.

Saul was one of the greatest persecutors of Christians before he himself knelt in repentance. We know him as the apostle Paul, the great missionary and the author of most of the New Testament. So don't fear hostile attitudes and actions. Who knows but that the person so antagonistic to Christianity is acting that way because they are coming near to it? An unhatched chick must struggle to break the hard eggshell that entraps it, and a butterfly must fight to tear open the cocoon that confines its new wings. When we see struggling in an unbeliever, we can imagine that barriers are breaking in the spiritual realm.

Even for believers, this turmoil before transformation can take place prior to spiritual breakthroughs and new growth. Realising this is a normal process can help us to understand and be patient with ourselves and to help others more skilfully.

Question: Are you, or someone you know, in a season of inner turmoil about some aspect of faith, some truth in the Word, or some personal habit or quality? How does knowing the process of turmoil before transformation encourage and equip you today?

Read: Acts 9:1-19; Proverbs 3:5-6

10

I AM FOR JESUS UNTIL DEATH

"This dear woman, a daughter of Abraham, has been held in bondage by Satan for eighteen years. Isn't it right that she be released, even on the Sabbath?"
Luke 13:16

Who are those our husband invited this time around? Mewau thought to herself. As the first and therefore senior wife of the three wives of Babu, she was concerned.

They had seen many visitors come to their isolated but large compound. However, these people looked different. They did not appear to be their husband's usual customers or those coming to drink wine, occasionally brewed in the compound for sale. Neither did they look like some distant relations arriving for the initiation festival that took place every 30 years, which was in a few days' time. Her mind churned, *Could they be the police? What had their husband done? Is any trouble coming to the family?*

Indeed, one could say that trouble was coming to her family in the form of change, but not in the way she feared as she arranged for the visitors to have water to drink.

AFTER-EFFECTS FOR THE WIVES

Mewau soon realized the visitors were there to tell her family about *Yesu.* Her husband, Babu, several visits later, expected her to convert. She refused until he agreed to go first. Then she followed suit, leading the way for the rest of the wives and children to convert as well. From all indications, Babu's three wives fell under the category of those who repeated the sinner's prayer out of loyalty to their husband. On his part, Babu did it because he wanted to make his family Christian, for none of the family members would agree to be in a religion which he was not practicing.

After that day, Mewau and the women started to observe whether their husband practised the new religion. But the man knew he was not sincere from the beginning, and the women were quick to notice this. They, too, started losing interest when they saw their husband's indifference. Only the children – including Koba – attended the teaching class we conducted in the compound.

The three women began to detest seeing us come to the weekly teaching in their compound. They thought we were idle people who only came to disrupt their work and to influence their children to become lazy. However, for the sake of their husband, they tolerated us even if they would not participate in the teaching. Babu rarely stayed home to attend the teachings. He was always out on business trips.

Mewau resented us the most. She had good reasons. She and the second wife, Araba, had kept several idols before Christianity's "intrusion" into their lives. Like most women in Kamuku culture, they were under the influence of a particular demon named *Sarauniya,* meaning *Queen.* Kamuku women were tormented by this particular evil spirit whose altar they built in their bedrooms. To this and other idols, Mewau and Araba made sacrifices of foodstuff, scents, fowls, and goats, depending on the type and time of the sacrifice.

When they became Christians, they were urged to surrender for destruction all their idols and items related to them. These included earthen altars, pots, calabashes, rosary beads, bottles, and white and red pieces of cloth. They declared in the name of Jesus that they had parted ways with them, in addition to declaring publicly that they now belonged to Jesus.

Mewau had peace of mind after surrendering her idols for destruction. However, this was short-lived. Soon she started having weird dreams. After each such dream, severe headaches set in. It was believed that those demons whose properties were destroyed were the ones tormenting her. She started to worry. She was advised to keep praying and binding those demons that appeared to her in dreams and to believe none of what they said to her. She prayed, but they kept coming. She could hear them threaten her.

In addition, her goats started dying one by one. Though she was the richest of the three of Babu's wives, soon all of her goats were dead. She feared she might die, too.

She lamented in the hearing of other members of the family: "This Jesus has no power to save me from this *Sarauniya* that is destroying me and my animals. What is the use of following him? After all, our husband who introduced us to the religion is no longer following it well."

She and the second wife, Araba, decided, "We are going back to the ways of our ancestors!"

BACK TO IDOLS

They rebuilt the altars they had destroyed before. They reinstalled new items representing those idols. They got more of all the things belonging to those idols and kept them at the altar. They began to sacrifice to *Sarauniya* and other idols, all of which represented demons. They also went back to drunkenness.

Their grown-up children, growing stronger in the faith, were not happy at this development. Their father, who was not serious with his own Christian faith, began to get concerned, though for selfish motives.

When they became Christians, the wives began to cooperate with him in running the family. But since they returned to their idols, he did not understand their ways any more. Therefore, he invited me to come and talk to "these women".

When I went to persuade them, the women had a ready answer. "Because our husband is no more in the faith, there is no need for us to continue," they told me. "Let the children continue with it, but for us, we are continuing with the ways of our forefathers."

Well, the children stayed, and their faith grew deep and strong. Their changed lives began to challenge their mothers who admired the changes they saw.

Meanwhile, the third wife, who was initially indifferent, finally saw the light and made a true commitment to the Lord Jesus Christ. She joined forces with the children, and they kept praying fervently for "our father and mothers who have gone astray". The young church, of which Babu's children formed the majority of the members, also joined them in praying for those and many others who seemed to have had a good start but fell along the way too soon.

For two years, God was working in the lives of Mewau, Araba, and Babu's family in general. These women observed with keen interest what God was doing in their family – inexplicable healings, less effort in labour during childbirth, and changed lives in the growing children. They also saw the true and practical love that the missionaries showed to the family.

Koba and Hayaya, the older sons in the family, who were married, were the most zealous and committed in the faith. In response to the changed life of Koba, her eldest son, Araba had to admit, "Even if Jesus did not come for the whole world, it is good that he came for my son."

In lighter moods, Babu would joke, "This 'thing' has really gripped the children very well." He would boast to outsiders and particularly to other Christians who, in his opinion, were not living rightly, "If you want to see true Christianity, come to my house."

Nevertheless, he remained unwilling to be a true Christian himself.

CONVERSION, TAKE TWO

No one could say for sure what made Mewau and Araba change their minds. However, one thing was certain: the prayers of the children and the church for those two women did not go in vain. The women started attending the daily morning and evening prayers with the children as well as the church service. This time around, they decided to follow Christ out of personal conviction, independently of their husband.

On their own, they decided to invite the church to come and destroy the idols they had brought back into their homes. The church gladly went. The women renounced those idols, broke the breakables, and burnt the burnables. One could see that Mewau was on a revenge mission on those demons as she broke the altar, the pots, and other items. She did this as if to say, *Enough is enough! You have had your worst; now is my turn.* With a similar zeal and a sense of finality, Araba followed suit.

Not long after, they were baptised. All could see that indeed a change came over Mewau. All who knew her could testify that her face glowed and her body looked fresher. Inside and outside, she was a new creation; the old had gone, the new had come (2 Corinthians 5:17).

When she had a miscarriage of a three-month-old pregnancy, people said it was the demons coming back. She replied, "This time around, let them do their worst, I am now for Jesus. There is no going back for me!"

Her prayer life became an encouragement even to the children who had prayed for her. Her attitude to the missionaries changed from that of hostility to friendliness.

"Before, I hated to see him," Mewau said, referring to me, whom God used to follow up on the family. "But now, anytime I see him, I feel as if I should 'swallow him up'" (out of love and admiration).

NEW THING BREWING IN THE HOUSE OF BABU

Ironically, Babu, previously unhappy that they returned to idols, became very uncomfortable and concerned about this development. He was already having problems with his children when they took their faith seriously. They would not compromise on issues of sin whenever he wanted them involved. Now his three wives all became serious, too. His thought they could be Christians but should still do anything he wanted them to do. However, the women thought differently.

For one, they were no more going to brew *burukutu* for him or for sale. People who used to troop to the house no longer went there.

The traffic had greatly reduced. Babu, unhappy, began to persecute both his wives and their children. He also began to avoid meeting the missionaries, whom he believed were responsible for dividing his family.

The test of the women's commitment came when sacrifices were to be made to the gods of fertility at the end of the guinea corn harvest. Babu had had a bountiful harvest that year, and each household was expected to brew the local wine. Many of Babu's non-Christian business associates had alienated him when his family became Christian. He, therefore, saw an opportunity to regain acceptance if he joined in thanking the gods by brewing drinks and offering all the required sacrifices. Babu was sure his wives would not disobey him in this respect. Therefore, he asked them to brew *burukutu* for the events, even if they were not going to drink it.

He got the shock of his life. They refused. "It is unChristian to do so," they announced. He was furious and threatened to "sack" all the three of them, by which he meant divorce. They were unmoved.

Mewau voiced how they all felt: "I am now for Jesus until death."

Babu contacted other women to do the brewing, but they all asked him, "What of your three wives?" Even his old mother and younger sister who were not Christians refused to help him. He resorted to using force on his female children to take the guinea corn for grinding at the commercial machine, fetch the water, collect the firewood, and do all the brewing for the *burukutu*.

Babu's aged mother pleaded with the women to reconsider their stand, as their husband would become a laughingstock. She asked them to consider if good wives should treat their husbands like that.

Mewau, as the senior wife, was the first to speak up. "Mama, you saw how the devil dealt with me when I was in his hand. Now I am in Jesus's hand, I do not want to go back to Satan."

Indeed, Christianity, not *burukutu,* was brewing well in the house of Babu.

Babu's three wives were all baptised and are still active in the faith. Several more of his children married Christians who are diligently serving the Lord. Some of his children who now have their own children are key leaders in their local churches. Babu's aged mother later became a Christian but has gone to be with the Lord in glory. Prayers are still going up that Babu will one day be restored to faith.

REFLECTIONS

The children wielded great influence in Babu's family, and the Lord specifically used them to help bring Mewau and Araba to faith. They were very excited at the first visit of the missionaries. When their father showed indifference and their mothers drifted too, it was they who attended the teachings we held in their compound, and their faith grew strong. Their fervent prayers were for "our father and mothers who have gone astray". Positive changes in the children provoked both admiration and a challenge to their mothers. Though their father was angered when his children would not cooperate with him in issues of sin, he nevertheless boasted to others, "If you want to see true Christianity, come to my house." Indeed, their good character, prayers, and consistency all exerted great influence on Mewau and Araba.

The wives observed that Christianity had no impact on their husband, and they drifted with him. But in time they observed its great impact on their children, and they followed suit. Who knows if they would have trusted Jesus if not for these children's example?

Let us not underestimate the influence that children can have in a family or community when they are the first to follow Jesus. At times, their faith is more trusting and more fervent than that of adults.

Question: Are there children in your family or church whom you are undervaluing simply because they are children? How can you give them opportunities to pray and to share the gospel?
Read: 1 Samuel 3:1; Matthew 18:10; 1 Timothy 4:12

In this story as in others, the new believer needed to smash, burn, and destroy their idols and all accompanying objects. It was amazing to see the zeal of both Mewau and Araba as they finally rid themselves of such demonic objects for ever. They seized upon their freedom like victorious warriors expelling an oppressor and reclaiming their homeland.

It was important in Kamukuland that the idols be destroyed openly for the family and community to see. Mewau and Araba invited the church to join them, and we gladly accepted.

The Bible talks extensively about idolatry as something God "abhors". In Exodus 32, we read how the Israelites, newly freed from cruel bondage in Egypt, returned to spiritual bondage by forming a golden calf. They bowed to it, danced, drank, and "indulged in pagan revelry". Moses was furious. He burned the golden calf and then ground it into powder. He destroyed its form, until it was no longer recognizable as any animal or object.

When the Lord sent the Israelites into Canaan, he said, "You must destroy all their carved and molten images and demolish all their pagan shrines" (Numbers 33:52). He did not say, "If there are beautiful bowls, feel free to re-purpose them for your homes. If there is colourful cloth, then be practical and make new clothes." His command was to destroy and demolish, without compromise. Where idols exist today, the same applies.

People may not always have physical idols in their homes, yet idolatry is still rampant. Idolatry is giving a place of high honour to anything that is not Jesus Christ. We may not realize at first that something has become an idol – a career, a person we esteem, possessions, sex, status, etc. We can grow accustomed to some idols in our lives, convincing ourselves they do not have power over us, but that we have power over them. Do not be deceived. You cannot "manage" a stronghold any more than you can "manage" a viper in your hand. The wise believer follows the example of zero tolerance and destroys them.

Question: Have you become tolerant of some of the idols in your life, and what steps do you need to take today to destroy and demolish these?

Read: 2 Corinthians 10:3-5; 1 John 5:21

11

THEY CAST OUT DEMONS

Then he appointed twelve of them and called them his apostles. They were to accompany him, and he would send them out to preach, giving them authority to cast out demons.
Mark 3:14-15

Like Babu's wives, many Kamuku women were bound to household idols and had altars built in their bedrooms to *Sarauniya*. Though the idols were represented by non-living elements such as stone, clay, wood, fabric, and straw, the powers behind them were very much alive and real. The women strongly believed that the idols controlled their lives, activities, and the well-being of their families, their property and prosperity. They worshipped these demons. They feared them and offered sacrifices to appease them. Some sacrifices were required on a weekly basis, others at the sighting of the new moon, while others were done as the seasons changed, and some coincided with another religion's time of celebrations. As Mewau and Araba found, these demons tormented the women when they failed to sacrifice at the right time. Punishments included physical illnesses, loss of animals, and weird or frightening dreams.

When Mewau and Araba first destroyed all their idols and the items related to them, the news of such a bold move spread in the region. More women wanted to part ways with their idols too! Though not intending to become Christians, many requested us to come and do for them what we did for Babu's wives.

The way to freedom was Christ. When they understood this, some believed. Those who believed were surprised by freedom. They were encouraged to part ways with the symbols of those gods kept in their bedrooms. Some willingly surrendered them for destruction. Others took a "let's wait and see if this new God is for real" stance.

There were yet some women who, though not willing to be Christians, wanted to be separated from their idols. They wanted rest from the sacrifices and hardships the demons made them pass through. They wanted to be free, too, from the wicked spirits but were not willing to accept Jesus Christ, the Truth that sets free. But without the power of Jesus Christ, freedom was not possible.

BICHI

Bichi had been coming to church. She had suffered much at the hands of such demons. She had spent much money trying to appease them and seeking healing from the illnesses they inflicted on her. In addition, they had humiliated her. When they possessed her, she would do many things without full awareness that she would be ashamed of later after the spirits left her. She wanted total deliverance from these wicked spirits and destruction of all their objects. At her invitation, we went to her house. We asked if she really believed in the Lord Jesus or if she just wanted to be delivered from the torment of the spirits. Did she want the Freedom-Giver or only the freedom?

Bichi lowered her head. In a low tone, she said, "What can I say? If I don't believe in Jesus, won't the evil spirits return again?" Bichi's confession, she then went ahead to break the altar built of clay and set fire to all the items on it.

It was our practice not to do the destruction. Rather, we prayed to neutralise all the powers of the demons and their influences on the woman. Then we asked her to uproot and bring outside the altar and all the items linked to it. Then we would ask certain questions, such as if she was willing to part ways with the idols and demons. Upon affirmation, she was asked to burn everything that could be burnt and break the breakables with her own hands in the presence of those gathered. After she was done, more prayers were said.

Bichi confessed, broke the clay altar, and set fire to all the items on it. The transformation that took place in Bichi was dramatic. The horrible dreams and nightmares that had robbed her of sleep every night for many years came to a stop. She continued growing in the faith and farming. She had been married before but was already single when the missionaries met her. Yet in her old age, suitors even started coming. However, she had made up her mind not to marry again.

We saw brightness in the faces of such women. People saw the difference it made in them. These changes that prompted other women to ask, "Come, help destroy our idols." They would say, "If so-and-so could be freed, whose demons are stronger than mine, then I, too, could be delivered."

BARALA

Everyone in the house loved Barala. She was the last born in her family and the favourite of her father. She was often the babysitter for one of her nephews. She would put him on her back and go places. She was fond of the boy because he was quiet, and she loved it that way. People saw in them a resemblance in character for she, too, was quiet and well-behaved.

She had carried the boy about on her back until one day when she was about 13 years of age. The boy's parents denied her his company, and she did not understand why. When she tried to carry him by herself, they took him away from her. She insisted to know why. They said, "Barala, you are not well."

"But nothing is wrong with me," she protested. Yet the people in the compound knew something had suddenly gone wrong.

Earlier in the day, Barala fell for no apparent reason. She stretched her body and yawned. Then she thrashed back and forth on the ground. They all saw it. The older ones in the family had their suspicions, but they wanted to be very sure before mentioning it by name. They feared the consequences of naming it.

Not long afterwards, it happened again. This time, even the children knew what it was: evil spirits had possessed Barala. They would come and throw her down. She would stretch and writhe on the ground. From then on as she grew up, the demons manifested in many ways.

Sand became her favourite "food". She would go to the stream and scoop out lumps of clay to chew and swallow. Sometimes she picked up pebbles and swallowed them. On many occasions she felt restless if she didn't eat sand after a normal meal.

Her parents went from one witch doctor to the other trying to exorcise the evil spirit. But the more witch doctors they consulted and paid, the more the evil spirits seemed to increase in number, and the more she suffered torment at their hands. When the spirits came upon her, they would raise her up and violently throw her down. She would convulse, foam in the mouth, and speak languages she had never learned, like Fulfulde and Gbagyi.

One day, Barala went to visit a friend who also happened to have some evil spirits. She had invited Barala for a feast of sacrifice which she had prepared to appease her own spirits. Barala went and the evil spirits in her grew enraged with jealousy. They wished she had done for them what her friend did for hers. For this, they threw her down and tormented her. "Why didn't you set up your own system of sacrifice for us?" they interrogated. When she returned home, she set up an altar.

From then on, added to her sufferings was the burden of sacrificing to her evil spirits as they demanded. Their torments became a "normal" occurrence, as they fell upon her from time to time. Eventually, she married and had two children. But she and her husband always quarrelled and fought. Barala had become a fighter, flying into fits of anger at any slight provocation. Her volatile behaviour became too much for the man to bear.

So she left their home and returned to her parents' house, where she continued fighting everyone who crossed her path. The evil spirits had transformed the once quiet and well-behaved girl into an argumentative and aggressive woman.

People would not come close to her. She had spent vast sums to get rid of the spirits. She was still young and aware that people knew she was possessed. No man attempted to marry her after the first marriage failed. In addition to being argumentative, Barala also became sad and lonely, tormented by spirits.

MISSIONARIES COME

When we started visiting to preach and teach in their compound, Barala detested us. I sometimes spent the night in the compound, and she would later confess that she had intense hatred for me. While others in the compound came to listen to our teaching, Barala would find excuses to leave.

Though she hated me the most among my colleagues, I kept going closer to her. Out of courtesy, she listened to me, though inwardly she boiled with anger. She was unwilling to become a Christian. Her excuse was simple: "I cannot. I will not be able to." And so she continued living as an unhappy woman.

But one day for no reason we could see, she began to show interest in the teaching times held at their compound. No one could say what attracted her. She simply began to attend. Seeing the door open slightly, her nephews who saw her as their elder sister began to preach to her.

By this time, she had seen many Kamuku women destroy their idols, and nothing bad had happened to them. She began to ask questions about the Christian faith.

Some time later, to the glory of God, she announced her desire to become a Christian. She accepted Christ as her Lord and Saviour, and she became zealous and serious. The evil spirits no longer tormented her. Her face grew brighter and brighter with passing days. She hardly ever missed Sunday worship. She was grateful to the missionaries for coming to deliver her. I, the one she hated intensely, became dear to her. She told someone, "Anytime I see him, I feel like swallowing him up!" (to express her love and gratitude).

After becoming a Christian, Barala became a cheerful, gentle, and kind woman. She was intelligent too, and it did not take her long to learn to read and write the Hausa language.

FINAL BATTLE

We had encouraged the new believers from CAPRO's work in Kamukuland to organise regular monthly meetings in Ukuru town, which was central to the various stations. So the members of far-flung congregations began to meet for fellowship and encouragement there. Barala attended one such meeting. All of a sudden, as the meeting was underway, she started shaking. She was lifted up and thrown down.

Demons can manifest themselves even in church settings; they did even in the presence of Jesus. For example, in Mark 1:23-24, a man possessed by an evil spirit cried out and identified Jesus even as he was teaching in a synagogue. In such a setting, an evil spirit can become very uncomfortable and upset, and therefore manifest itself.

Barala foamed at the mouth and began speaking in languages she did not know. Some in the congregation understood what she said, and according to them, her words were not edifying to those gathered (1 Corinthians 14:4). They suspected, therefore, that the evil spirits had returned to abuse her.

After she spoke, she was left unconscious. The congregation went into prayers for her. They bound and cast out the demons. The demons cried aloud in response. They left with a great deal of noise, using her voice. Afterwards she came to her senses, unaware of what had happened to her.

From then on, Barala continued her life as a Christian, to the surprise of those who knew her as a demon-possessed woman. Later she attended the Discipleship Training School in Bango in Katsina State. There, she learned how to sew clothes. She returned and volunteered as a cook in CAPRO's primary school in Maruba station. Later she went to CAPRO's Hausa School of Missions, and then went to work as a missionary among another tribe.

Two explanations could be given for the demons' return after she professed to have become a Christian. One is that quite a number of people become "Christians" by just mental assent or head knowledge, without a heart conviction to personally appropriate the complete work of Christ on the cross as sufficient for their total salvation. In Nigeria, there are many reasons why people become "Christians". Often these reasons are the fringe benefits Christianity offers. In any of these cases, one with evil spirits can be tormented whenever the atmosphere is not comfortable for the evil spirit, such as the church environment Barala found herself in during the prayers.

A second explanation is found in the example Jesus gave in Matthew 12:43-45, in which an evil spirit leaves a person but finds no new home: "Then it says, 'I will return to the person I came from.' So it returns and finds its former home empty, swept, and in order. Then the spirit finds seven other spirits more evil than itself, and they all enter the person and live there. And so that person is worse off than before."

Jesus is describing someone who found temporary relief from the presence of an evil spirit, not lasting freedom in the presence of the Holy Spirit. Such freedom comes only through repenting and welcoming the Lord into one's entire life. In contrast to the Matthew passage, the Bible describes Jesus saying, "Look! I stand at the door and knock. If you hear my voice and open the door, I will come in, and we will share a meal together as friends" (Revelation 3:20).

Being a true Christian is only not about the absence of evil; it is about the fullness of the presence of the Lord. Without it, a swept, orderly, and vacant house is an invitation for any potential occupiers to come in. And what demon who is evicted will come back alone and risk re-eviction? Rather, he will go and find more and stronger demons to join him in possessing the house more securely than before.

REFLECTIONS

Demons are real. Their presence and activities among human beings are real. We must not mistake our inability to see danger as an indication that there is none, or that there is no such thing as demonic activity. This is what the Devil would be happy for us to believe. Anyone who does not believe in the reality of demonic activity in the world today will have to contend with the Bible.

Demons, like their father Satan, always harm and hurt humans. Barala was forced to eat sand and pebbles. Bichi was inflicted by an illness. Many Kamuku women suffered the oppression of sacrificing to demons. The boy in Matthew 17:15 was thrown into the fire and water. The man at the tombs cut himself with sharp stones (Mark 5:5). Demons can make their victim convulse, shriek, and speak unrecognisable languages, or they can render a person mute, as they did to Dariya (chapter 2).

Therefore, we must not be careless or casual about the power of demons. Satan prowls, patrols the earth, and watches for opportunities to attack (Job 1:7; 1 Peter 5:8). He does not announce his plans. We see this when the manifestations of the evil spirits in Barala's story, as in others, came suddenly "out of nowhere". Thus, we are warned to be on the alert.

In Ephesians 6, we learn how to wear the armour of God to protect us in the fight. We must keep our faith alive and growing, for the Bible compares our faith to a shield which protects us from the fiery darts of the enemy. Prayer and God's Word are some of our most powerful weapons, weapons Jesus himself used against Satan and demons. So, too, we must use them to protect ourselves and to free those held captive by the enemy.

Question: When you are reminded of the reality of demons and the victory of Jesus, how does it affect your prayer life? How can you put on the full armour of God today?
Read: 1 Peter 5:8-9; Mark 9:17-29; Ephesians 6:10-18

Demons are as real today as in Jesus's day, and so the power of Jesus's name to cast them out is as real today as it was in Jesus's day. Jesus is the same yesterday, today, and for ever.

Though evil spirits must obey us, we must not delight in this. Doing battle in the spiritual realm is necessary to the Christian life, especially in missionary endeavours, but it is not the centre of our life any more than cleaning a home is the purpose of the home. We must be highly skilled and trained yet maintain a kind of disinterest in it; be highly alert, yet never over curious. An elephant is equipped to kill a hunter skilfully with one kick from its massive leg. Yet no elephant spends its days seeking hunters to kill or dwelling on its own lethal power. As Christians, we, too, exert our authority whenever it is necessary to bring freedom to the oppressed, but our focus is not on this authority. Instead, our focus is on the joyful hope that spiritually freed people will have their names, like ours, written down in heaven!

Question: Where would you put yourself on a scale with casualness towards demons on one end and excessively dwelling on them on the other end? How can you move towards the balance of an elephant – powerful and alert to danger, yet daily focussed on walking with God and with other believers?
Read: Luke 10:17-20; Mark 3:13-15; Mark 1:21-27

12

AUTHORITY OVER SNAKES

You will trample upon lions and cobras; you will crush fierce lions and serpents under your feet!
Psalm 91:13

One Sunday, the church's presiding elder, Gamaiwo, woke up earlier than usual, for he had much to do. He was excited and had good reason to be.

Today, for the first time since the planting of the Kangon Biri church, a local believer, not the missionaries, would baptise the new believers in the river – and he was that local believer. Thereafter, he would conduct the Communion service. After the service, the whole church would go to his house to feast.

Gamaiwo's wife and other women were overseeing the food that morning. Gamaiwo sent his younger siblings to catch and slaughter some chickens and guinea fowl for the meal.

The children were delighted to chase the fowl. It was fun. But up to the time Gamaiwo was leaving the house for church, which was some kilometres away, they had caught none. Seeing their helplessness, he alighted from his bicycle to assist. Satisfied that they had the number of fowl they wanted to slaughter, he went again for his bicycle.

He had one foot out of the grass. Before he could lift the other foot, something terrible pierced him. Pain shot up his leg. He was stunned and motionless for some moments. Slowly his mind cleared. He was facing a viper! Fortunately, a stick was handy, and the snake paid with its life for biting him. He went back into the compound and relayed what happened. His father inspected the spot and confirmed he was indeed bitten by a snake.

The family dispatched his stepbrother to go and inform us on the mission base of what happened. When the brother arrived, we were getting ready for service. We exchanged the usual greetings, which included asking if everything was well back home. As was the custom, he answered all the questions affirmatively. Only after this did he tell us that a snake had bitten Gamaiwo.

In that moment, I recalled when Gamaiwo had first become a Christian and how we had wondered if his faith was real. Surely now it would be tested.

"So," I thought out loud. "This snake has gotten a member of the church at last."

TESTIMONIES

The local congregation, every Sunday service during testimony time, was full of stories about God's protection and provision. Chief among the testimonies was that of God's protection from snakes. Somebody had either held or stepped on a snake unknowingly, and it didn't harm them. Some dangerous snakes were discovered in the bedroom or lying on the road but got killed. Hardly a Sunday passed without a testimony of God giving victory over snakes.

We, the missionaries, also testified that were it not for God, snakes would have sent us packing out of the station, dead or alive. They came in dreams and real life. My wife recorded killing five in a week when she was left alone on the mission compound. Three times, big cobras were killed in our bedroom. On one occasion, my wife and I slept with a cobra "guarding" us at the head of the bed. We woke up, and I left early for another mission station. As my wife was sweeping the room, she discovered our "night guard". She had killed snakes before, but she did not think she could handle that big cobra. The snake, too, raised its head but then went back to its rest. My wife went to look for help.

When others arrived, the snake knew its match had come and went on the offensive, spitting in someone's eyes. People were surprised that the eyes of the brother did not go blind. God saved those eyes, for his glory.

The mission compound and those of the believers were surrounded by bushes. So, I did not attach any spiritual meaning to the snake incidents. Some worldviews err by not believing in the reality of demonic powers, while others err on the side of believing that demonic powers lie behind everything. Even a bird flying accidentally into an open window may cause shouts of "Depart in the name of Jesus!" This second extreme gives rise to many superstitions.

I did not want to assume evil behind the presence of snakes any more than one might assume evil behind the presence of mosquitoes if one lives near a swamp. But one day, a visitor made us begin to consider whether there were some spiritual connections.

The man was a trainer from the School of Missions in Gana Ropp who came to supervise students on their mission field exposure. After only his first night, he called me and began to tell me about sensing the presence of extraordinary snakes around. I laughed and told him he might be right. Then I began to narrate our experiences with snakes, both real and in dreams. The visiting missionary was alarmed. "Bro! We must do something about this," he said. "It is not normal."

Indeed, it became clearer to us that it was not normal. In every testimony, the snakes had been killed before they could deliver their venomous bites. But now, Gamaiwo had been bitten.

ONE WEEK; TWO INITIATIONS

The fact that Gamaiwo was the person who had finally been bitten by a snake seemed to have some significance. From the very moment of his conversion, threats from other spiritual powers had targeted his faith.

Only a couple of years earlier, Gamaiwo had professed his faith in

Jesus. It was at the time when all males in Kamukuland 30 years and younger were to be initiated into the Magiro Cult. The initiation took place at the shrines on the Uregi Hills, the people's ancestral home. This was also an opportunity to show the new generation where their forefathers "sleep".

Gamaiwo secretly did not want to go through with the ceremony. When his father asked him to take me around the scattered settlements, he confided, "I wish my father would decide quickly that all of us become Christians before the ceremony begins." The ceremony had already begun for other clans, but Gamaiwo's clan still had a week to go.

Then at last, with barely a few days to go, the father made his decision: he asked that all members of the family convert to Christianity. Gamaiwo and almost the whole family was led to Christ. But this didn't go down well with Gamaiwo's uncle and other neighbours. When they understood that the conversion meant the non-initiated members of the family would no longer go to the shrines, they were angry with Gamaiwo's father. "How can you say that the children cannot go and see their ancestors?" They pressured him until he gave in.

Although he refused to go to the shrine himself, the children, including Gamaiwo, were tricked into helping the elders just to carry the food meant for the ceremony. When they reached the hills, they were forced to stay until the ceremony was over. Thus, within a week, Gamaiwo was initiated into two different ways: Christianity and the Magiro cult.

Because of this, we began to doubt the genuineness of Gamaiwo's conversion. People like him should not have allowed themselves into the cult, for they had professed Christ.

To Gamaiwo, he was only doing the wishes of his elders, whom tradition says should not be disobeyed for any reason. In his mind, he said he had become a Christian. So, upon returning from the hills, he and others who had professed to be Christians yet went to the shrine apologized to us.

We had almost given up on the whole family. In fact, we stopped going to teach them for some time. But God had his plan for the family.

It seemed he overlooked their ignorance. And he caused us to have a change of heart. We resumed teaching in the compound.

Looking back now, we expected too much too soon from the family who knew next to nothing about Christianity until their mass conversion just a few days before the ceremony.

"IMPOSSIBLE" CHALLENGES

Following his conversion, Gamaiwo continued to encounter challenges that tested his faith – and our patience. He was slow in learning how to read and write. Attempts at teaching him were frustrating and discouraging. He seemed to have made up his mind, complaining, "It is not possible. I will not be able to."

But he was not a complete write-off. He seemed to value the spiritual and moral lessons taught him. They suited his naturally quiet and gentle disposition. While he saw nothing "possible", he would still go ahead to try at whatever he was asked to do. Though he would do it well, he lacked self-confidence and was full of condemnation for himself. At a point, he gave up on learning to read completely. I gave up on teaching him too.

Some months later, I saw Gamaiwo reading the Hausa Bible fluently. "How did he do it?" I asked.

"God so helped me," he replied. Truly, God was the only patient teacher Gamaiwo had. For when I, the human teacher, had given up on him, Gamaiwo turned to God in prayer. He would come back the next time, knowing what he had once claimed was not possible for him to know.

Gamaiwo still had problems recognising numbers. So, I set out to teach him to count in Hausa. Numbers 1 to 100 were written on a blackboard for Gamaiwo to learn. In the first session, Gamaiwo learned to count up to 39. I wanted the lesson to stop at 40. But Gamaiwo could not go further than 39. I would add 40 for Gamaiwo to repeat. But Gamaiwo would say, "I will not be able to." What the difficulty was in just mentioning 40 after 39 was a wonder! I was annoyed and closed the lesson. Gamaiwo was embarrassed and never turned up to continue.

A few weeks later, Gamaiwo was leading the Sunday worship service. He asked the congregation to open to Psalm 100. I happened to be in the service and was surprised. *What did I hear? Did the man have a pre-opened passage to Psalm 100?* No! Gamaiwo opened to it before anyone in the church could find where Psalm 100 was in the Bible. He had learned and could recognise numbers one to 100.

"How did it happen?" I asked Gamaiwo later.

He smiled. "So, is it only you the Holy Spirit teaches?" I blushed with shame. I agreed with Gamaiwo, the Holy Spirit could teach anyone anything. But the precise way the Holy Spirit taught Gamaiwo how to count from 1 to 100 remains a mystery to me.

Through these experiences, Gamaiwo learned to pray and to rely totally on the Lord for his needs. Eventually he grew so strong in his faith and in his knowledge of the Word that when we handed over the church to the local people, we appointed four overseers, with Gamaiwo as the presiding elder.

WHAT SHOULD WE DO?

Now Gamaiwo, a new leader intending to baptise and serve Communion for the body of Christ for the first time, had venom in his veins. *Would his faith survive this attack? Indeed, would he himself survive?*

And what would we do? It was costly to treat snake bites in hospitals. Snake antivenom was not easily obtained. The nearest hospital was more than 100 kilometres away. In that context, by sending a family member to inform us, the family was saying, "A snake has bitten one of you. What are you going to do about it?" If not, the hospital would have been the first place the family thought of.

Well, we decided to pray. Was it the only thing we could do because we believed in prayer or was it a panic measure? Or was it a cover-up for our inability to do anything? Could we help by taking him to the hospital? But who would bear the cost? We, too, had no money to undertake such a gesture.

Maybe we truly believed God would heal the man. Whatever it was, prayer was the only thing we could think of at that moment. So, the three of us in the mission station and some church members who had arrived from their various settlements held hands and began to pray for Gamaiwo.

Just then, Gamaiwo arrived on a bicycle! Following a snake bite, it is better to remain still. Movements such as walking or pedalling a bicycle will help to speed the venom's spread throughout the body. When Gamaiwo's stepbrother had left for the mission station, Gamaiwo told the other members of the family, "I know they will be praying for me now, so I better go and join them." Before anyone could advise him against it, he had pedalled the whole distance from his house to the mission compound.

He joined the ring that formed to pray for him. During the prayers, he started feeling dizzy. He sat down. The prayer continued. After the prayer, did everyone believe it would work? Maybe Gamaiwo did. Maybe some of the believers did. And maybe one or two of the missionaries did too.

I felt the prayers needed to be "supported". Before the brother had arrived with the news of Gamaiwo, I had actually been thinking of a shock treatment that was administered to me when a black scorpion had stung me seven months ago. Maybe the memory of the shock treatment had come to me prior to the arrival of the news because I was supposed to use it now. So, I suggested that it be given to Gamaiwo. *It had worked for a scorpion sting. Would it work for a snake bite? There is no harm in trying.* Some missionaries in other parts of the world had used it before, and I had read about it in one of the mission magazines.

Fortunately, there was a motorcycle around. We disconnected the plug from the wire that supplied its power. The naked end of the wire was placed on the spot the snake had bitten. The motorcycle was kick-started several times to let the current pass through Gamaiwo. It was painful – I knew that from experience. But I insisted on several more kicks against Gamaiwo's shout of "*Ya isa!* (It is enough!)"

Despite this drama, when all the believers arrived, the baptismal service went ahead at the nearby river. Gamaiwo stayed on the mission compound to rest.

"Snake!" someone shouted. They had been watching the baptism from the far side of the river. Those on the side of the baptism looked around. Right there a big, brown snake had meandered from the bush, head raised and poised to strike. The snake was pursued and killed. The baptism continued.

When the believers returned from the river, Gamaiwo's leg was swollen, his eyes were reddened, and he felt weak and dizzy. His parents and relations grew alarmed. Some believers began to express concern. We began to fear, *Is he going to die?* This was the question on everyone's mind. *If he died, what would people say? Would we be charged for negligence or manslaughter? Would the enemy turn this day of celebration of new life in Christ into a day of mourning over death?*

The church went for the Communion service, leaving Gamaiwo alone under the cool shade of a tree. After the Communion service, Gamaiwo's condition worsened.

Whispers started to swirl. "He should have been taken to the hospital," some said, without saying who should have done so.

The parents looked on helplessly. Their son was dying, slowly and painfully. When the father could no longer bear keeping quiet, he spoke up. "We think he should be taken to the hospital. What do you think?" Again, he did not say who should take him to the hospital.

"Well, you can take him if you want to," I replied. "Though we feel that the prayers will work, and God will heal him."

"Well, he is in your hands," the father resigned. "You know what is good for him. After all, he is your son too."

Neither of us were categorical or committal. We both had our fears. The parents feared the cost of treatment in the hospital, though they wished him taken there. On the other hand, we believed in God's intervention, but also couldn't help fearing that the young man might die in our hands. So, we would be glad if the parents took him away.

During these uncertainties, Gamaiwo was not moved. He laid quietly listening to the conversations and the whispers. The leg continued swelling and paining him. However, he was the one that settled the matter.

Asked if he wanted to go to the hospital, he was emphatic. "No! The prayers made this morning are enough. I believe God will heal me."

Come to think of the wisdom of asking a patient to decide if he should be taken to the hospital or not. If for nothing else, at least that freed us from responsibility. We now knew who to blame should he die in our hands.

WILL HE DIE?

The day continued. Gamaiwo's wife and mother were asked to return home. Then the church went to have the meal in his house while he rested at the mission base.

The father stayed back with him. He and one elderly man in the church, a former witch doctor, still felt that something needed to be done. The ex-witch doctor brewed some concoctions from black soot and other unknown ingredients and brought a bowlful for Gamaiwo to drink. He explained that it would make him vomit the bad blood formed in the body. Though they knew Gamaiwo's faith suggested he should refuse, he had demonstrated obedience to his elders around the time of his conversion. Perhaps in such desperate circumstances he would comply again. But to their dismay, Gamaiwo refused to drink.

The first day came to a close, and Gamaiwo did not die. The faith of the believers was strengthened. He stayed with the missionaries, and the believers prayed in their homes. The unbelievers expected to hear at any moment that he was dead. Some believers took time to come and keep him company in the day. The swollen leg was continually massaged with broad fresh leaves warmed over live charcoal. On the third day, he began to stretch his leg and even put it down.

On the seventh day, Gamaiwo walked from the shade tree to the church, healed. He gave thanks to God and testified of his healing power. Later, he walked home a healed man.

Hearing that Gamaiwo was out of the mission's compound healed, some unbelievers concluded and thus spread the rumour that I must be a wizard to have treated snake bite without medicine.

But the believers knew *who* did the healing in answer to their corporate and individual prayers. When Gamaiwo was asked why he had refused the concoction of the former witch doctor, he said, "They would have said it was the drink that healed me."

The following Sunday, almost everyone in the church had one thing or the other to say in appreciation and thanksgiving to God for healing "our pastor". Gamaiwo stood to thank God for healing him and the people of God for standing with him in prayers. His concluding words were: "This happened to me so that God's name will be glorified."

Another incident made us consider whether the snakes had some spiritual connections. One night, I dreamed of a big snake laying trapped between two logs of wood. As I brought out a knife to cut its neck, it turned into a human being, not recognised by me. After that dream, the incidents of snakes in the mission compound reduced drastically and seeing snakes in our dreams also stopped.

To the glory of God, no other snakes ever harmed either the missionaries or the believers the whole time we were in the field, despite many close encounters.

REFLECTIONS

Everyone thought it was impossible for Gamaiwo to survive the bite of a venomous viper. But Gamaiwo had seen God do "impossible" things before: he learned to read and he learned his numbers. Conquering smaller "impossible" challenges as a new believer built his faith, so he could look back on how God had delivered him before. When you are tempted to doubt, remember what the Lord has done for you in the past.

You can also look to the Bible and remember stories of God delivering people from seemingly impossible situations. In Acts 28, the missionary Paul was also bitten by a viper and survived. He was on his way to Rome to stand trial before Caesar when his boat was caught in a dangerous storm that last for days. The sailors were sure they would die, but God did the impossible. He saved the lives of the entire crew and they made it safely to shore! When they reached the shore, Paul was bitten by a viper. The islanders first thought it was a sign of God's judgement and expected him to fall dead. No such thing happened. God did the impossible again. It was God's plan for Paul to arrive in Rome, and nothing could stop it.

Remembering God's character in the past will lend you courage in the present and fortify you with peace for the future. When the forces of nature threaten us, remember God is their Creator. When the forces of evil threaten us, remember Jesus has defeated them. God's plans will prevail. He is the same God today, yesterday, and for ever.

Question: When has God brought you through seemingly impossible times in the past? How can you grow your faith in God by remembering with gratitude his past deliverance?
Read: Acts 28:1-6; Psalm 77:11-13; 1 Chronicles 16:11-12; Luke 10:18-19

One way Gamaiwo proved that his faith had grown to a level of maturity was in the way he handled the situation after he was bitten.

Others who were older than Gamaiwo or in positions of influence or authority were undecided about exactly what to do. At many points, he could have pleaded with the missionaries, his parents, or other church leaders to choose the way for him, assuring them of his submission to whatever they chose. Many would have seen this as appropriate and even honouring. But in this case, God gave Gamaiwo knowledge of the way to go, and Gamaiwo directed everyone into it. If he had relied on others, they may have arrived at the same decision he did – not to go to the hospital in light of the great distance, great cost, and no guarantee of success – but then the Lord would not have been glorified in Gamaiwo's response of faith.

When his faith had been brand new, Gamaiwo went in ignorance to the initiation of the Magiro cult; but now with seasoned faith, he proved that he could refuse, despite excruciating pain, even a small bowl of concoction from an ex-witch doctor, offered quietly out of the public eye. As a new believer, Gamaiwo practiced relying on God in small challenges in private, as a mature believer he faced big challenges in public during a crisis.

Gamaiwo did not rely on others' faith for him; he now relied on his own faith in Jesus. As he said, "The Holy Spirit can teach anyone anything." While we weighed this outcome and that outcome, Gamaiwo sought one outcome: the glory of God. His faith not only resolved our indecision, it paved the way for God to be glorified. However, then he had to continue in this faith, living it out day by day through pain and discomfort, until he was fully healed.

Question: Are there times when you take the easy route of relying on others to make decisions for you, decisions that you know God is revealing to you the right way to go?
Read: Hebrews 5:14; 1 Timothy 4:12

13

WHEN HE DRINKS A DEADLY POISON

"These miraculous signs will accompany those who believe: They will cast out demons in my name, and they will speak in new languages. They will be able to handle snakes with safety, and if they drink anything poisonous, it won't hurt them. They will be able to place their hands on the sick, and they will be healed."
Mark 16:17-18

It was curiosity that drove him. The teachers of his own religion spoke evil of Christianity. But Samu kept wondering, "If that religion is so bad, how come those who practise it are good? When you are sick, they take you free of charge to the hospital. When you have a need, they are always ready to help. They are kind. They care for one another. Moreover, they seem satisfied and happy with themselves." All these troubled his mind.

The opportunity came when Samu met one of the teachers of his religion in a big town. He saw it as safe ground to ask the pressing questions on his mind. He summoned courage.

"Excuse me, sir, please, don't be angry with me. I want to ask you a question."

"Go ahead," the teacher smiled, wondering what an audacious young man he was.

"Which of the religions, ours or theirs, really leads to God?"

The teacher looked sternly at this strange inquirer. *What a question, and what boldness!* Looking the young man straight in the face, he said, "You want to know the truth?"

"Yes, sir," the young man answered.

"Well, I will tell you the truth, but don't say I told you. The Christians are on the right way to seeing God."

Samu returned home with more questions on his mind. "Then, why are we not taught this? Why is there abuse and persecution of those who are on the right path? And why was his teacher still in that religion?" The teacher told Samu he had not left because he would lose his livelihood as a religious teacher.

Samu was loved by the other young men in his religion. He was active as a member of a vigilante group set up to watch over the community. He gave himself to the study of the great book of his religion. Yet he remained troubled and kept asking, "Which religion saves?"

One day, he was in the company of his brothers weaving grass for roofing. Suddenly, he was transfixed by something the others could not see. A fire was raging. He was being drawn into it. But a missionary who had preached to him in the past was trying to drag him out of it. When he recovered from that trance-like experience, he told his brothers. They thought he was going out of his mind or was being possessed by some evil spirits.

After their work, he went to see the missionary he saw in the trance. He inquired more about the way of salvation. The missionary shared the gospel with him and led him to Christ.

TROUBLES BEGIN

That was the beginning of Samu's troubles with his father, his wife, their extended family, the vigilante group, the elders of his community, and the people of his religion.

At first, his father did not take him seriously. Samu's elder brother had once joined these people, but he left not long after. He thought Samu would not stay long either. But Samu was different. His zeal in the new faith was contagiously provocative. A few weeks after his conversion, he was preaching repentance in his own words to all that came across him. His new faith and lifestyle troubled his father and some of the elders.

His father was a sorcerer who worked and practised with demons. Samu's father knew that a "strange" power had entered his house. Not only did the power enter but whatever it was, it was nullifying his own powers. Something needed to be done.

At first, the father tried to persuade Samu to renounce his new faith. But Samu refused. Instead, Samu grew bolder and more assertive in his evangelism. One target he did not spare was the falsehood behind Magiro worship, which he exposed to non-initiates. This made the elders furious with him.

The father resorted to using some of his diabolical powers. On several occasions, Samu's portion of food from the central pot of the big compound was poisoned. Samu would come and, without knowing, pray and give thanks to God before eating, as he had been taught. On one occasion, the very young members of the family informed him that they saw their father putting something in his food. Samu ignored them and ate his food anyway. On yet another occasion, two of his elder brothers who had poisoned the food stood by to watch what would happen to Samu. To their dismay, they saw Samu pray before eating. One of them was terribly angry and shouted, "Samu, why must you pray before eating?"

Seeing the superior power of the Spirit in Samu and that Samu's continued stay in the house was a threat to his practice as a sorcerer, the father decided to take more drastic actions. He invited another sorcerer from the faraway area of Birnin Gwari in Kaduna State to join forces to deal with this disobedient son of his.

The man came on the appointed day. The father was out drinking somewhere, so the visitor met Samu with his newly married wife. Samu made the visitor feel at home until his father returned. His wife brought drinking water and he brought out a mat for the visitor to relax. The visitor was impressed by this young man's hospitality. When Samu asked if all was well, he decided to confide in him his mission.

"Yes, your father asked me to come so that together we could deal with one of his sons who has gone astray." He went on describing the offences of that son.

"I am the strayed son," Samu told him upfront. The man was shocked and embarrassed. Samu went on to rebuke the old man, asking him to repent of his wickedness or perish. The visiting sorcerer could not stand this "small boy" preaching to him. He packed his items of trade and left.

On his way, he met Samu's father returning home. "I have been to your house," the man said without completing the rounds of the greetings. "I didn't know the young man I met in the house was the erring man. He was good to me and I told him my mission. I am leaving because what that young man told me really pierced my heart."

Samu's father was speechless. "So, this boy is going out of control."

The next day, he travelled to see a religious spiritualist of one faith to seek his help against his son. The man agreed to make an incantation from his great book. The incantation was said to bring calamity in whatever form of adversity the person wished on the named target. The fee was settled, and the religious spiritualist sat to invoke the spirit that would harm Samu, according to the father's wish.

But something strange happened. The first and the second invocation "went into the air". That is, the evil spirit could not locate Samu, its target. The man was alarmed. Samu's father saw it in his face.

"Is it all well?"

"No!" the religious spiritualist said rudely. "This boy you want to harm is innocent. The two times I have invoked, and the spirit went into the air. If I invoke for the third time, I am afraid it will bounce back to either you or me. But I am sure it will be you, because you are the one wanting to harm somebody."

Not satisfied and still wanting to destroy his son, Samu's father visited yet another religious spiritualist, more famous than the former, at Kampanin Bobi, along Minna-Kontagora road. He presented his "problem" and all the efforts he had made to solve it.

"To be honest with you," the religious spiritualist started, "if I want to cheat you, I can ask you to pay much money for nothing. The truth is that if the young man is a true Christian, there is nothing we can do that can harm him."

However, the father insisted that he didn't mind being "cheated." He asked the religious spiritualist to do his best. They travelled back to Samu's village so that the spiritualist could see the young man. Perhaps his divination could work at close range. The man went and did his best, returning richer with some fowls and money. Samu remained unharmed just as the religious spiritualist told the father. Samu was truly a Christian.

Samu was aware of his father's moves to destroy him. He saw some evidence for himself, and other people told him, "This is what your father has done or is planning to do." Samu was not moved. He would report the warnings to the missionaries and the church to help him pray.

When spiritual means failed to harm Samu, his father incited all the other members of the family against him. The large family, including the father, three married sons and all their families, farmed and fed together. Samu was forbidden from farming with the family. He didn't mind, yet the father did not leave him alone.

One day, Samu bought groundnut seeds to plant, and his father poisoned them. The seeds turned completely black. Samu planted them all the same. A few days later he reported, "They germinated as if they were planted with fertiliser." He continued to work hard on his own farm with his wife.

WOMEN TURN AGAINST HIM

Finally his wife began to turn against him too. She said she did not marry him as a Christian, since he had become one a few months after they wed, and therefore she would not stay in his house unless he renounced his faith. Taking advantage of Samu's now gentle nature, she would beat him at the slightest provocation. It seemed she was demonised just to deal with Samu. She once confessed to a missionary, "I don't know why I beat him, because each time, I feel full of regrets and sympathy for him." But she did not stop.

On one such occasion, her father-in-law himself had to intervene saying, "Do you want to kill my son?"

Samu and his wife had what was called an *exchange marriage*, a type of marriage contracted to avoid paying heavy dowry. Dowry in the culture was as high as ₦200,000, besides many goats, tens of fowls and bags of guinea corn. So in this arrangement, two women from different families were exchanged as dowry for each of their brothers marrying from the other family. (That is, if I want to marry your sister, my father will give your father my sister for you to marry; then neither family has to pay dowry. But in that arrangement, if my wife ever leaves me, then your wife, who is my sister, will have to leave you too.)

One day after beating Samu particularly harshly, she left Samu and threatened not to return to her father's house. Samu's father understood what that threat meant. If she just disappeared, Samu's sister who was exchanged for her would not return to the family. That would be a great loss since it would mean he had given his daughter in marriage for free. Samu's sister could only return to Samu's family after her exchange counterpart returned home.

So, the father asked Samu's elder brother and Samu to ensure that Samu's wife, who was set on leaving, was handed over to her parents. They obliged and forced her home to her family. When they arrived and explained what happened, Samu's in-laws began to verbally abuse him, to which Samu's elder brother had to defend Samu because Samu could not answer his in-laws back.

Back in his family, the persecution continued. One day Samu's mother called him. She did what Kamuku children most feared. Looking at him and raising her flabby breast upward, she cursed, "If you were fed from this breast, you will soon begin to wander about in the bush." Interestingly, when the father heard about the curse, he was not happy with his wife. In their tradition, that curse was irrevocable. However, weeks passed and Samu did not go mad.

One day, Samu had gone for a church service a few kilometres away from his village. In his absence, some believers from other mission stations visited to encourage him. They waited, but when Samu did not return on time, they left.

As soon as they left, a woman in the household went up "into the *bori*" (the demons possessed her) and began to prophesy. She said, "The *church* has come to stay in the compound and there is nothing anyone can do about it. But if they trouble the *church* too much, the *church* will go away. They would look for him but would not find him. But the *church* will come back after some time."

When Samu neared home, the *bori* said, "The *church* is now coming back, and he must not meet us here." Then they stopped talking and departed from the woman. She fell into a deep sleep.

When Samu entered the compound, he found the woman sleeping on the ground in a distorted posture. He asked, "Why is she lying like that?" The others explained everything to him.

TRIALS

The scope of his persecution continued to expand beyond the family and the immediate community. One day members of the vigilante group reported to the local chief that he no longer reported for duty. He was tried and found guilty. As punishment, he was asked to be on night duty for two weeks nonstop.

Samu had decided after becoming a Christian not to work in the group any more. According to him, some of the things they did there were ungodly. So, he refused to report for his punishment. He was summoned and asked why he had not come. He said because the chief had threatened previously to lock him up and spray tear gas in his eyes. The chief was furious and said Samu lied against him. Samu maintained that this threat was what the chief said.

The chief ordered Samu to be locked up in a goats' house. He was served food the next morning. When he ate it, his stomach started grumbling and burning, and his entire body started itching.

My family lived in a nearby mission station. Someone crossed the river to tell me about Samu's detention. I immediately went to see the chief but met only his deputy and his scribe in the chief's court. Setting formalities aside, I went straight to the point.

"I understand one of my brothers is in detention. What did he do?"

"Oh! He has gone home," the deputy replied.

"But what did he do?" I insisted.

"It is a small matter," the scribe said.

When Samu returned home, the father was angry. He did not expect his release so soon or to see him alive, for that matter.

Then his elder brothers conspired to tell a lie against him. They went and told the local chief that Samu had burnt some portion of their religious book. They believed Samu would be killed for the sacrilege.

Samu was summoned to the big village where the local chief and many who belonged to that faith lived.

"Why did you burn the great book?" someone asked.

"How could I?" Samu fired back. "You people say that fire cannot burn the great book, so how could I have burnt it?" No one said anything. The crowd, poised to lynch him, was disappointed.

Though they allowed him to go, a plan was hatched to waylay and assassinate him along the road. The father gave the plan his blessing. An informant told Samu of the plan.

One of my team members followed up to encourage him to remain firm in the faith. Samu said, "I am ready to die rather than to renounce my faith. Even demons have confirmed that *church* has come to stay in this house!" Indeed, and despite the pressure, Samu had made up his mind – there was no going back.

A SEASON IN HIDING

The threat on Samu's life became intense. Finally, Samu had to leave home to an undisclosed destination. He left in such a way that could not be linked with any missionaries working in the land. All of us were on the field the day he left. But the locals believed we arranged Samu's sudden disappearance. They naturally thought he was taken away to Jos, the capital of Plateau State, as the locals believed that all of us serving in that field came from there.

But Samu was not far from home. He lived among a nearby tribe where he was nurtured spiritually. He became such an encouragement to both the local believers and the missionaries he met there.

There he learned much and burned with zeal and appreciation to God for saving his life. "Sometimes, I feel I am the only one God loves in this world. But when I think of my people who are still in darkness, I feel like crying," he told me when I visited to see how he was doing.

In hiding, Samu devoted himself to learning how to read and write in Hausa. He hired himself out to work on people's farms, saving enough money to buy a Bible. He wrote to his father to tell him how much he loved him. The father began to pester us to bring back his son. We ascertained his sincerity and asked Samu to return.

Samu returned from his hiding and continued to show practical Christian love to his family members, especially to his father. He would collect and wash his father's clothes, get him water to bathe, and do menial things that his siblings, both younger and older than him, would not do for their father. The heart of the father began to soften towards Samu. He began to confide in Samu some deep things he had not told anyone before.

When the father fell sick, it was Samu who took him to the hospital and stayed with him. On his sickbed, he apologized to Samu for all the wrongs he had done to him. Samu assured him he held no grudge against him. Samu talked to him in the hospital and prayed for his salvation. He died in Samu's arms, a peaceful man.

The *church* indeed came back home after a year, and he became a pillar in it. He married a Christian lady. Both went to train in the CAPRO's Hausa School of Missions, and they now serve as missionaries among another tribe.

REFLECTIONS

Samu's father, his mother, a sorcerer, and two famous religious spiritualists tried to curse Samu and failed. He was innocent, a true Christian, so they admitted, "There is nothing we can do that can harm him." The superior power of the Holy Spirit in Samu was nullifying his father's spiritual powers.

In the Bible, we also see King Balak hire Balaam, a famous pagan diviner from a far-off land, to curse Israel. Three times Balaam tries and fails. He says instead, "No curse can touch Jacob; no magic has any power against Israel."

As Christians, we do not need to fear curses, evil spirits, or demons. Jesus, through his death on the cross, has defeated the powers of evil and shamed them. Although they keep fighting to take captives, their ultimate destiny has already been decided. We have access to that same power that raised Christ from the dead, and it is stronger than all other powers and dominions! No demon nor evil power can ever separate us from God's love.

Question: Think of a time when you or someone you know has been afraid of curses or evil spirits. What biblical truth can give you confidence in God's power?

Read: Numbers 23:7-8, 23; 24:1-13; Romans 8:37-39; Ephesians 1:18-21

Samu faced persecution on every level – spiritual, physical, and social. Spiritually, there were demonic attacks by his father, a visiting sorcerer, and other spiritualists. Many physical attacks came in the form of poisoned food, cursed groundnut seeds, banishment from farming and eating with his family, and imprisonment. But the third type of persecution may have been the hardest. His mother cursed him. His wife beat him and deserted him. His father blessed a plan to kill him. His family spread lies, hoping to bring about his death. His friendships with other young men turned hostile.

But Samu remained unashamed of the gospel and willing to suffer for it. Though he was living in the body among his earthly and painful circumstances, he was living "by faith in the Son of God" (Galatians 2:20 NIV). Jesus reminded us that the world hated him first (John 15:18). He also promised us that if we are persecuted for righteousness' sake, then we are blessed and will inherit the kingdom of heaven (Matthew 5:10-11).

Question: Are you living in fear of persecution that may come or has already come? How can your perspective be transformed so that though you live in the flesh, you also live by faith?
Read: Romans 1:16-17; Galatians 2:20; Matthew 5:10-11

14

BROUGHT BEFORE KINGS

"You will be dragged into synagogues and prisons, and you will stand trial before kings and governors because you are my followers. But this will be your opportunity to tell them about me. So don't worry in advance about how to answer the charges against you, for I will give you the right words and such wisdom that none of your opponents will be able to reply or refute you!"
Luke 21:12b-15

It had been a few years since Baba Dogo had revealed that Magiro was nothing but a gang of men masking themselves and hiding undercover to visit terror and fear upon non-initiates. Baba Dogo had not been "swallowed up" by Magiro for his defiance, contrary to everyone's expectations.

But Magiro continued to wax stronger, even though some of its followers have embraced Christianity and another religion.

"This is the way of our ancestors. How can we leave it and follow another way?" its followers would often retort when Christian workers preached to them. "Our ancestors will be unhappy with us. They will visit us with calamities like sicknesses and poor farm produce if we forsake Magiro," they would argue.

The missionaries and their prayer partners' constant prayer request was "that the strongholds of Magiro over the lives of the people be broken." After I left the field, my colleague felt emboldened to dare the gods.

The young missionary, Samson Mancha, had been thinking to himself: *If Magiro is nothing but a means to intimidate women and perpetuate the dominance of men over them, if the revelations so far indicate that Magiro is not even an idol but merely a concept of terror, and if the people could be told the truths, maybe there would be a breakthrough in the work of the missionaries.*

He was zealous for the Lord and quite young, as were most of the missionary team and the new believers. He believed in calling a spade a spade when it came to spiritual things. No compromise would he permit with the way of the world. He wanted to confront evil directly.

For some time, he had pondered how Magiro must be confronted to break the mystery surrounding it and to free people from fear. Then he came upon a brilliant idea: *What is done secretly in the nooks and crannies of rocks in the Uregi Hills should be reenacted on the open plain where all the people can see. What is done secretly by men must be seen and heard by women and children. Magiro must be stripped naked.*

But as an outsider, he didn't know much about what went on in the hills during Magiro worship. How could he expose what he didn't know? Then he thought, *The emerging new churches planted by CAPRO have enough young men who came out from the cult. They will know more.* So, he contacted elders and leaders from each of the churches and presented his idea.

It seemed good to them. In fact, most of the young men had been preaching to their own people trying to convince them of the deceit in Magiro worship and to reason why they needed to become Christians. To them, this new idea would deal a final blow to Magiro, and its adherents would see the light. They agreed wholeheartedly to the suggestion to expose and disgrace Magiro publicly. But it was not without one or two dissenting voices.

Suajo, usually one of the more radical and fearless young men, had a word of caution, "If we do this, we will lose the people and therefore block our way to evangelism." Monphile, another fiery and fearless believer, agreed with Suajo. But they were in the minority, just two out of the twelve Christians selected from the five churches. When their advice was not taken, the two joined the majority despite their different opinion, and there was unity among them.

Thus, as one body, the machinery was set in motion to unmask the god.

PREPARATIONS BEGIN

Those who had reached a higher level in the cult before becoming Christians were asked to recreate the instruments that constituted the voice of Magiro and the voices of the ancestors.

Magiro's "voice" was breezing and whooshing sound. This was created by carving a piece of flattened wood into the shape of a sword blade, with a hole at one end. A rope was tied to the wood through the hole, and the other end of the rope was held tightly and swung around clockwise to produce strong whooshing sounds. Complementing this was a wooden flute weighed down by a ring of gum in the middle with fiery red bead-like seeds from a fruit tree. Several holes were made below. Then a gong was made by pieces of iron struck one against the other.

Next they created the ancestors' "voices", which were less like a voice and more like a throaty sound. The throaty sound was supposedly because "death has eaten the mouth of our ancestor". A short, hollowed corn stalk was sealed at one end with spider's paper, a round and thin encasing tissue found on walls and leaves. Blowing softly through the hole produced the throaty sound. The last instrument was the cover of a wild orange-like fruit with two opposite holes in the middle and which gave a whistle when air was blown from the other opening.

Having improvised all these, a date was set for the great showdown between the Kamuku gods and the Christians. It would be a Sunday.

The 12 believers converged at Kaya station on the appointed day. The choice of Kaya might have been informed by the fact that Samson resided there or because Kaya was close to the range of hills that housed the shrines of the gods of the Kamuku clans.

Prayer and fasting took place the whole day. As they broke the fast in the evening, the heavens opened and showers of rain poured down. Was God blessing the action that was about to take place? Was he trying to soften the ground for the great fall of the gods whose falsehood was about to be laid bare? Whatever the reason, the rain benefitted the believers for after it ceased, a great stillness hung in the air. Whatever message the believers had for the gods and their adherents would be heard loud and clear; it would travel greater distances than it would have had it not rained that evening.

The leader announced over a megaphone powered by a dry cell battery, "We are here to expose and tell you about Magiro. Those who do not know should come and see Magiro! We are prepared. If you are a man, come prepared. A blind man does not ask a sighted man to play with stones unless he has stepped on one. So, we are ready. Today is the day to tell you the truth. We are inviting everyone – men, women, and children. Come and see!"

This proverb Samson used was an expression of confidence from the side of the Christians, i.e., the "blind man". They were blind as to what went on during Magiro worship in the hills. While the Magiro worshippers may have interpreted the "stone" in the proverb as a physical weapon, the Christians had no such thing. Rather, they had some knowledge of what went on secretly in the hills and above all, they had great faith in God. Thus, these introductory remarks – or psychological assault, if you may call it that – set the stage for what followed.

SPECTACLE IN THE FIELD

The command was given. The flute started, and the singing wood answered. The metal gong joined and the gods "cried". Soon the ancestors joined the crying gods. The megaphone carried the weeping of the gods far beyond Kaya into the settlements and clustered compounds scattered along the fields and hillsides. The priests and all the people heard it.

"Abomination! Incredible! So, these children meant to carry out their threat," the high priest muttered to himself. He was yet to recover from the shock of his son becoming a Christian. He had been grooming him to take over his position.

But Magiro continued to "cry", and for no special occasion. "This madness must be stopped. Those stubborn children and the missionaries must pay dearly for this."

The men were agitated. They were earlier sent indoors by the heavy downpour. Now, though it was still drizzling, they had to go out to stop this mockery of Magiro.

The men came from various directions of the scattered settlements and beyond the River Kaya. Each came with a deadly weapon – guns or bows and arrows. When they came, they found that Magiro was crying in the most unlikely place – in the field in front of the mission compound! Worse still, their eyes confirmed what their ears had heard: it was not the custodian of the Magiro who called. Rather, it was a set of the "rebellious" children who had abandoned the ways of the forefathers. The men were enraged, full of contempt and hatred that fuelled a desire to avenge this desecration of the gods.

Darkness was gathering as men arrived. For some strange reason, no one attempted to do anything to any of the believers scattered on the field enjoying the fun. Instead, they began to congregate in front of the nearest compound that faced the mission base and the field where the Christians were busy mimicking their gods.

"Oh, if only Mr So-and-so were around, we would have dealt with these children already," one man lamented.

As if waiting for his name to be called, the man whose name was mentioned appeared. True to their expectation, he began to scold those who arrived earlier. "What are you waiting for? Get up! Let's deal with these children once and for all."

"Be careful!" an elderly man cautioned. "Don't go near these children anyhow or they will finish you off. You don't know what they are carrying."

Indeed, the psychological assault on the people earlier was having its intended effect.

"These children must have indeed stepped on 'stones' to dare us. They must be having some deadly weapons to deal with any man who comes near them," other men thought aloud in agreement with the counsel of the elderly man. The men's fear stemmed from a rumour going around that after I left Kamukuland, I kept in touch with the believers by supplying them with guns. No such thing happened. But the rumour was enough that they warned men who came later.

Someone among the crowd asked angrily, "So, why are we gathered here like rain-beaten chickens?" Soon they began to disperse in the direction each came from.

The believers had no weapons of war. Their confidence lay only in the fact that they had prayed to God the whole day. They believed he was on their side. So they dared the gods and their adherents in open confrontation.

When the men dispersed, the youthful Christian men stopped the imitation of the Magiro cry. They were satisfied that they had passed their message in clear terms. Some of them left that night to their respective villages.

But the Kamuku men were not done yet.

RETALIATION

They regrouped the next day to plan their line of attack against the Christians. They decided to take up the matter with the Local Chief, who was not a Christian. Determined to deal severely with the rebel children, they taxed each household who worshipped Magiro ₦3,000 to enable them to pursue the case to the highest level, if need be.

When the case came before the Local Chief, he denounced the Christians without hearing their side of the case. He told them they should reject their actions and admit they had done wrong. The believers, however, refused to admit to doing any wrong.

Later, however, the Chief and his local council later tried to absolve Samson of blame, hoping to distance the outsider from the case in order to deal exclusively with the locals and intimidate them. But Samson stood with the believers, saying, "It is true that they are the ones who know the secret of Magiro and therefore exposed it. But if you say I have no fault, then these ones, too, have no fault, for we are together. They are my people."

"Then this case is beyond my power," the Local Chief told his council and the crowd that gathered to hear the proceedings. So, he sent the case to the District Head.

The District Head is a kind of king in his own right, residing in a walled palace from where he rules and holds court. More crowds gathered at his palace than at the place of the Local Chief. People from all over Kamukuland had come. Adherents of both the Magiro cult and another religion had joined forces to see these Christians wiped out of the land. Even a Catholic priest was found and brought in to testify that the believers had acted wrongly.

Like the Local Chief, the District Head sided with the Magiro worshippers and denounced the believers for rebelling and disobeying their parents. He also gave them little to no chance to defend themselves. All the people pronounced them guilty and now demanded their deaths. Samson was accused of leaving his homeland to come and "knock together the heads of these children with their parents". But the believers stood their ground even as tensions ran higher and higher.

The chief threatened to hand them over to the police for torture. The crowd called again for their heads. But according to one of the 12 men, "We had already sacrificed our lives. We were ready to die."

When the young believers refused to budge, the District Head changed his tone, "Now kindly, go and apologise to your parents and settle this matter at home. But if you don't, the Emir himself will have to hear this."

The emirs of northern Nigeria are traditional rulers who serve as both political leaders as well as custodians of Islam in the emirates over which they preside. Although there are government institutions such as the police and civil courts, often the emirs wield more power and are closer to the people and culture. They often hear cases that have more to do with the customs of the people.

So Samson conferred together with the 12. "What do you think about the advice of the District Head?"

One of the believers said, "If we withdraw at this point and apologise, we will be in for more trouble. Let us all speak with one voice and maintain our position to the end of the matter."

Another added, "If we back off at this point and apologise, we would have to pay heavy fines for the sacrilege committed against Magiro. The people will demand repayment for what they spent up to this point. They will exaggerate the amount just to punish us."

So together the believers stood their ground and refused to plead guilty.

THE EMIR'S SUMMONS

About two weeks later, the Emir sent his summons. The appointed day arrived, and both the believers and their accusers travelled a long distance to appear before him.

A still larger crowd gathered in the Emir's spacious palace complex than in the District Head's. More Kamuku and non-Kamuku people from other regions of the land milled about to witness the downfall of the Christians.

The Emir's council took their seats. When His Royal Highness emerged from his chamber, all including the Local Chief, the District Head, and other dignitaries bowed low saying, *"Ranka shi dade.* (May you live long.)" The 12 believers clustered together on one side, separate from the huge crowd. Every indication around the court suggested that the matter had come to a terrible end in favour of the idolaters.

The accusers had spent much money on these trials. They now hoped to avenge their gods by seeing the Christians killed, believing the Emir had the power to order such killings.

Back home, mothers and wives of the "children" were crying and mourning. "They have taken them to the big town to be killed."

After the Emir took his seat, he looked at the 12 young men and the multitudes arrayed against them. The court was quiet. He adjusted himself on his seat. In a matter-of-fact way, he said, "Do not be afraid, young men; this case is going to be over today." The silence intensified.

He addressed the believers again, "Tell me, why are you fighting your parents?"

Monphile, one of the two who had originally dissented from this course of action, was now their spokesperson. He said, "We are not fighting our parents, your highness. We were only trying to let them see the truth, but they refused to see." He went on to narrate what happened.

"Then, let me hear the pastor. Where is the pastor?" Samson indicated he was the one. "Give way to the pastor," he motioned to the Local Chief.

Samson stood and thanked the Emir for the opportunity to speak, unlike at the two previous places. He said, "Before, we were denied speaking." At that, the Local Chief and the District Head, both sitting on the floor before the Emir with many others, began to shift uneasily. They tried to hide their faces before the Emir's questioning gaze.

Samson told the Emir why they exposed Magiro. "It is a false god. Women are kept in bondage by it. We want them to be free. We want them to know the truth."

The Emir had listened to the case. Without wasting time, the verdict came: "You are free to go and continue preaching your religion, but don't impose it on others. We want peace in our land. So please go and don't make trouble again."

The turn of events was so sudden that even the Christians were caught unaware. The Local Chief began to complain, "Your highness, there are five churches in my domain. There are too many, and I want some closed to leave only one for effective supervision."

The Emir asked, "How many did you say?"

"Five," the Chief answered.

"Then they should go and build three more if they can, to make them eight," the Emir said with a sense of finality.

The Emir's palace singers went to work celebrating the triumph of faith in their own way. They swayed over to where the 12 were seated. "The Emir has released you," they shouted jubilantly. "You have been granted favour. Go in peace."

The believers stood and marched joyfully with shoulders held high to the utter dismay of their accusers. The heads of their adversaries were bent in shame and humiliation. When they came out of the palace, the believers found a spot and together, they lifted their hands in thanksgiving to their God who fought on their behalf. The others walked away without so much as a word to one another.

Like Rev Tuller, who had arrived 80 years earlier, Samson Mancha wanted to expose the false gods, to open the eyes of the Kamuku people so they might turn "from darkness to light and from the power of Satan to God" (Acts 26:18). Both used the same strategy – harnessing the knowledge of new believers who knew the secrets of the cult in order to expose the falsehood of Magiro worship. Both used unconventional means but achieved different results.

What the Rev Tuller started in the 1920s had grown in full course and had now blown up in the face of the descendants of those who had once opposed the gospel. You may call it the folly of zeal, youthful exuberance, a triumph of faith, a daring gamble, or the humiliation of kings. Whatever it was, God glorified himself, not only before the few Kamuku believers, but before non-Kamuku people and unbelievers too.

REFLECTIONS

This story confirms what Jesus said about his followers being brought before kings who were hostile to his cause. Jesus's promise to believers who find themselves in such a situation was also fulfilled. Without putting up much of a defence, they were discharged and acquitted, so to speak. As we see the world growing more antagonistic to Christ and the gospel, this story will continue to be enacted.

A power showdown like this that provokes or shames one's enemies is, and should be, very rare. However, a well-known story in the Bible parallels this confrontation between God and idolaters. It took place in 1 Kings 18:20-40, led by the prophet Elijah against the prophets of the idol Baal.

Elijah had called the false prophets and the people to Mount Carmel on an appointed day. He challenged the people of Israel gathered, "How much longer will you waver, hobbling between two opinions?" He went on to introduce the contest that is about to take place. Similarly, the missionary Samson laid out the nature of the challenge at hand – a public exposing of the truth. Both men set the stage by announcing the truth challenge at the centre of the event and inviting the idolaters to come and watch. What courage it must have taken to instigate and to host such a spiritual battle. Once the words were spoken, there could be no turning away. The event could not be stuffed back into a bottle.

The scene on Mount Carmel surely looked quite lopsided. The 450 prophets of Baal stood on one side while Elijah stood alone on the other. One side was sponsored by the royal family of Israel, the other by the God of Israel. At Kaya station, the Magiro adherents stood on one side, backed by the tribe's priests, elders, and traditions; on the other side was a Christian minority, led by a foreigner with no local status or power, but backed by the Almighty God.

The people were silent after Elijah spoke and the Magiro worshippers at the field also held their tongues, but their ears had opened wide to the question put to them: "Do you really have the true God? Together we will find out today."

Question: Are you in situations today where the Holy Spirit may be prompting you to step out in faith with a truth challenge into a sin-filled situation?
Read: 1 Kings 18:20-24; Matthew 10:16; 1 Peter 3:15

Samson the missionary and th[illegible]ng Kamuku believers appeared before the Local Chief, the District Head, and finally the Emir himself. In Acts 21 to 28, we see another story of a missionary on trial whose case escalated to higher and higher courts: Paul. In Paul's story, we see how each escalation provided a new audience for the gospel – both Jews and Gentiles in three different cities. In Jerusalem, he spoke to the crowd as he was being arrested and then to the Jewish court, the Sanhedrin. Then he was tried in Caeserea in front of the Roman governors Felix and Festus, as well as King Agrippa. Finally, he appealed to Caesar in Rome, and was able to preach to Jews in Rome, whom he had eagerly desired to meet but had been prevented.

Samson originally wanted to confront Magiro worshippers in the villages within the reach of his megaphone. He was not trying to get arrested. Yet God, in his providence, used this persecution like an even bigger megaphone for the message. Because the men were tried at higher and higher levels, and eventually the Emir's palace, both Kamuku and nonKamuku people from the surrounding regions heard the news that Magiro was powerless.

When we try to share the gospel and we get a negative reaction, sometimes we may need to re-evaluate our tactics. But we shouldn't always view opposition as a sign to back off. Indeed, God may use that resistance itself for his purposes.

Question: Where have you hesitated to share the gospel because you are afraid of opposition? Ask the Holy Spirit for wisdom and boldness to share with whatever audience he grants you.
Read: Acts 23:11; Romans 1:13-17; 8:31-39

15

A CHURCH OF MISSIONARIES

> Whenever I pray, I make my requests for all of you with joy, for you have been my partners in spreading the Good News about Christ from the time you first heard it until now. And I am certain that God, who began the good work within you, will continue his work until it is finally finished on the day when Christ Jesus returns.
> Philippians 1:4-6

Six years after my family and I left, I attended a combined service between the Kangon Biri church and its church plant in Ukuru. During the announcements, my presence was recognized. "We just want to say thank you for your labour amongst us. We love you and want to say good-bye."

I stood up to wave at the people and noticed how much the church had grown. They had built a bigger building for the church than the first church, roofed in zinc by prayer. What a contrast to the old Green Cathedral! Some of the old people and small children had come from long distances – some elderly women even crossing the river – to formally bid me farewell. I thought of Dariya's grandmother and Baba Dogo. I was glad Christianity was a "children's thing" but also embraced by the elders.

When asked to greet the church, I tried to say words of encouragement. But I couldn't contain myself. I sobbed when I thought of what God could do in the lives of people using a nobody like me. Seeing the brilliant transformations in such lives was enough for me to shed tears of joy and gratitude to God. The kingdom of God had expanded in their hearts; the labour had outlived me.

Following the church service was a love feast. The church had slaughtered a goat and some fowls. Plenty of rice was served. We sat to eat and drink *kunu*. We talked and reflected on the times we were there.

The next day I was to leave, and the church sent one of the elders to give me some money, "For your transport." It was more than I needed for my fare back to Jos.

SUPPORTING MISSIONS

A few years after leaving Kamuku, a church elder approached me during a conference and handed me a brown envelope. "It is from the Kangon Biri church," he said.

"What is it for?" I asked, thinking the church wanted me to help them buy some books or evangelism materials.

"It is for you. The church has decided to start supporting your family." I was overwhelmed with gratitude both to God and to the church.

Just as the believers in the early church in Antioch sent money back to the mother church in Jerusalem (Acts 11:29-30), so this new church plant was giving generously back to the ones who helped to plant it. Since then, they have continued to give us cash or gifts in kind, as the occasion warrants. I was touched one time when they bought and transported about 50 tubers of yams to us.

The Kamuku church also materially supports teams of indigenous believers who continue in evangelism and church planting among their own people where CAPRO missionaries leave off. In one year, they collectively gave these teams about ₦1,000,000 in addition to food.

The churches in Kamuku are also reaping the fruit of their generosity. They are prospering materially, among others. Even just four years after we left, they had roofed all the houses with zinc besides the two we did before we left. The station had a television and a generator. At a conference, I observed many participants from Kamuku were bright looking. Two came with their personal vehicles, a car and a pickup truck. I could not help but ask my friend Koba, "What is happening that most of you are looking so fresh?"

He replied, "*Romon bishara ne.* (It is the additional benefit of the gospel.)"

SENDING MISSIONARIES

I visited the church again in October 2017 and in April 2019. The young boys and girls we left are married and blessed with their own children. The believers we left are still standing and growing in the faith. The indigenous churches had been handed over to the local people. The churches they led shone across the land "like lights on a hill" among the different clans of Kamuku – Tureghi, Azubazuba, Ţucindo, and so on. The two local churches in Kangon Biri and Ukuru are growing in number.

When we came as church planters, we were hesitant to provide a zinc roof so the church would not be seen as *our* church, the "church of the missionaries". But today, they are a church of missionaries – themselves! Kangon Biri has since planted two daughter churches, and the Ukuru church, now relocated to Anguwan Tanko, has planted one. All five churches are led by people originally from the Kangon Biri church.

Eight missionaries made up of three couples and two ladies have gone out from the Kangon Biri church the last time I checked. One of the two ladies is now married to a missionary from another station.

On the apostle Paul's second missionary journey, he met a young man, likely a teenager, named Timothy, who would become his apprentice in the Lord. The relationship of father-son and teacher-student grew into a relationship between co-labourers and brothers.

As the apostle Paul discipled Timothy of Lystra, so the apostle John took young Ignatius of Antioch to disciple in the ways of Jesus. Two decades later, a white-haired Ignatius and young Polycarp walked a similar road. Two millennia later, such unbroken chains of teachers and students continued, up to the time John Hall and Gordon Beacham brought the gospel to my people, the Tangale, in the 1920s. Three generations later, I took it to the Kamuku. And now I see this grace flow on from these believers forward to new peoples and generations.

Even now, I feel the unbroken chain flowing past me like a current of the Lord's strong will that is too wonderful for any one life or any one generation to contain. It is the great plan of salvation for the world unfolding surely, steadily, beautifully, until the earth is "filled with the knowledge of the glory of the Lord as the waters cover the sea" (Habakkuk 2:14 NIV).

YOUR PRAYERS CAN MAKE A DIFFERENCE

As I mentioned at the beginning of the book, today the church in Kamukuland in particular, and the people of the land in general, are under attack by bandits and terrorism. They are left in a tight and sorry situation. After one deadly attack that forced the people to flee their homes, one of the displaced persons and a Christian leader wrote:

> Some of us are now living in rented houses in the town. Many are overcrowded in small spaces because they don't have money to rent their own spaces. Many don't have money to feed themselves. We have to buy water and firewood to cook. [Things they once obtained easily and for free in their natural settlements.] Both adults and children now fall ill often and are unable to go for treatment in the hospitals. We now look up only unto God, who is our sole hope, to intervene in the situation we find ourselves in.

After fleeing, some people started returning to their homes and farms, which raised the challenge of how to feed and to farm that year. In the previous attacks, their food supplies were either stolen or destroyed, and they had no money to buy farm inputs. This prompted a mission leader to raise the following prayer alert:

"Let's pray and raise help for them to settle down again when farming starts, even as we raise help to feed them now." He added, "Thank you for standing with the terrorized and traumatized people of Kamuku and other tribes."

Similarly, another missionary who worked in Kamukuland reported in early 2022: "Our people are virtually stranded now that the farming season is fast approaching. Everyone seems to be asking, "What does the future hold for us?""

THE REASONS

Many questions have been asked, most urgently, *What exactly do the terrorists want?* Individual analysts, keen observers, political and religious leaders, and the Nigerian government have given different and sometimes conflicting answers to this question.

In some parts of the country, the terrorists have made clear that their goal is to wipe out Christianity and the existing system of government in the country in order to replace it with a system they believe is ideal for all humanity. However, in the course of time, their activities have deeply affected both Christians and non-Christians.

In other parts of the country, it appears that the terrorists, who are mainly of a particular tribe, are on a mission for territorial conquest. It is believed they want to take over the country, which they believe is their possession. Here their strategy involves impoverishing the people, dispossessing them of their land and livelihood, and subjecting them to a form of slavery. They use the poor peasants to finance their activities through ransom, taxes, and levies. This seems to be the case playing out among the Kamuku and other people groups. In such situations, both Christians and non-Christians are victims of violence, kidnapping, abduction, rape, maiming, and mass murder.

Another popular position is that what is happening is religious persecution of Christians. Proponents of this opinion cite instances when Christians are the primary victims of forceful mass abductions, plundering and destruction of property, and mass murder. Credence is lent to this position by the government's silence or inability to bring the perpetrators to justice when Christians comprise the majority of victims. When the perpetrators are very clear about their targets and intentions, then we rightly cry "persecution" and pray, "Lord, behold their threats!" However, when the attacks are politically or economically motivated and adherents of all faiths are attacked, then the violence is not categorized as persecution.

POINTS FOR PRAYER

Any time I hear that people – irrespective of tribe, region, or religion – are being terrorized and traumatized, I cry out in prayer, "God, have mercy!" Anytime I hear that a community with a majority of Christians has been attacked, I ask myself, *Is this the long-awaited, inevitable persecution that all Christians must pass through?* (2 Timothy 3:12). Please take a moment to pause and join the church in Nigeria in prayer. Here are some ways you can pray, in addition to however the Lord leads you.

- That the Nigerian government will step up to its responsibility to provide security to its citizens.
- That God will change the hearts of the perpetrators of evil, cruelty, and injustice, so that they will, firstly, stop these acts and, secondly, accept the love of Jesus Christ for them.
- For the urgent needs of food, medication, and accommodations for the victims of terrorism in Kamukuland and other parts of northern Nigeria.
- For Christians in Nigeria to stand true to their faith and bear testimony to their Lord amidst the horrendous situations they find themselves in.
- That the larger body of Christ will come to the aid of the displaced Christians to meet their material and other needs.
- That Nigeria will begin to know peace again, for the sake of the spread of the gospel within and outside its boundaries.

PRAYER WORKS

Your prayers make a difference. In answers to the prayers of God's people in Nigeria and beyond, we have been spared prolonged grief in all that is happening to the church, the land, and the country. Many of those abducted or kidnapped later regained freedom under varying conditions. Though they were treated inhumanely by the bandits, God spared their lives and brought them out safely. Though the people of the land suffered great losses in human lives, animals, and property, they are yet gradually picking up the pieces of their shattered lives and dreams.

I wish to thank all who stand with the scattered Kamuku church, the people of the land, and the northern tribes of Nigeria who are being harassed and terrorized. Thank you for your prayers and support.

> We always pray for you, and we give thanks to God, the Father of our Lord Jesus Christ. For we have heard of your faith in Christ Jesus and your love for all of God's people, which come from your confident hope of what God has reserved for you in heaven. You have had this expectation ever since you first heard the truth of the Good News.
>
> This same Good News that came to you is going out all over the world. It is bearing fruit everywhere by changing lives, just as it changed your lives from the day you first heard and understood the truth about God's wonderful grace. (Colossians 1:3-6)

LETTER TO A YOUNG MISSIONARY

Dear fellow missionary,

It is heartwarming that your obedience to the Lord has brought you into pioneer or frontier Christian mission work. How gratifying that young people like you are willing to take up their cross, follow Jesus, and do all that he tells them to do. It is encouraging to know that you sacrificed and left your all in obedience to Christ's command, "Go and disciple the nations." May the Lord depend on you.

With almost 30 years of serving as a cross-cultural, frontier missionary with Calvary Ministries (CAPRO), I testify that God is faithful to keep his promises to those he has called to serve. God's faithfulness has been our theme as a family. We have experienced in real terms his love, mercies, grace, and, goodness in different ways. What Jesus said about gaining one hundredfold what we have left to follow him (Mark 10:28-30), we have found a reality in the course of our ministry. In fact, our hearts' cry and prayer has become, "God, grant us the grace to justify your spiritual and material investment in us as a result of launching out in faith to work with you."

If you read my book *I'd Rather Die on the High Ground*, I am sure you have learned from our successes and failures. The experiences narrated in this book are true life stories that I was privileged to witness. I am sometimes surprised that God could use even me to be part of what he did in Kamukuland within the short time of our ministry there. It is a mystery I cannot explain. But it is a thing of joy to have witnessed those miracles of God in the lives of people once in darkness now brought to light, worshipping and glorifying God. I am also humbled that God in his wisdom decided to reveal his strength and power in my weaknesses. The key factor in our achievements is our availability in the hands of God. God makes able those who are available to do his work. In this work, after having faithfully played your part, you will need to look less to yourself for results and more to God and what he alone can do.

Sometimes I am tempted to look back at my work with trepidations or concerns. Here I am often filled with retrospective wishes. I think of many opportunities missed for evangelism that would have produced great results. Certain things to have done differently for greater effectiveness and impact. Some relationships to have built or strengthened. More commitments to have made that would have expanded the work. More daring activities to have engaged in that would have sent the devil to flight. And the list of such wishes could go on and on. But there is danger in dwelling on the negatives instead of seeing God's faithfulness and thanking him for the much he did through our yielded and feeble efforts. One can achieve anything at any given time only with the grace God gives at that time.

I am still learning that, as one grows in one's walk with the Lord, one's capacity for God's work expands proportionately. God's grace supplies strength and wisdom enough for his work at any given time. Through regular self-evaluation and examination, see to it that nothing of self or sin in your life frustrates God's sufficient grace for any given assignment at any given time.

Missions, I have come to learn, is about people. God so loved the world of people, he sent his one and only Son to save people. The Saviour loves the people of the world and came down to earth, willingly died to save humans from sin and to reconcile us to God. In that vein, we ought to love the people of the nations we are sent to reach out to. People should be our focus and the reason for our being on the field. If we lose sight of this, we will likely end up expending much energy and resources doing many things but soul-winning.

I am ever grateful to God for his gift of teams. He values teams and teamwork. Hence in his dealings with the universe and humanity he has always worked in a team as the triune God. It is therefore never by chance that he places us in teams we find ourselves to work with. I truly enjoyed mine in Kamuku and the other places I have worked as a missionary. I still enjoy working in teams. You may find this very important when you consider that no soldier fights alone and wins a battle. Frontier mission work, as any aspect of Christian life is a battle. Your team members are your greatest assets to help you succeed in your work outside other resources God has endowed you with. My counsel is to devote enough time and space to interface in a Christian manner with your team members. Work for their well-being and progress in their spiritual and ministry growth and development. Your team members include both those you work with closely and those supporting you in one way or the other from afar. Always pray for both categories and wish them well.

Prayer played a key role in our work in Kamukuland, as you can read in the book. This can never be overemphasized in the life of a Christian, and that of a missionary in particular. The thrust of the book is that God works his work through his servants who are weak enough to rely absolutely on him through prayer. Your life and ministries should be soaked in prayer alongside the Word of God. My experience is that if for any reason a missionary becomes weak in one or both, his life and ministry are finished. Beware that these are two main areas the enemy of the gospel attacks most frequently.

Your call as a missionary is a great and noble one. I tell myself and all that care to listen that if I had the chance to live another life, I would still choose to obey God by working as a missionary. So don't let anyone look down on you because you serve God as a missionary. You are not inferior to anyone serving God elsewhere or in other occupations. Nothing gives me greater joy than the realization that God found me worthy to be called to work with him in this particular area of ministry. That God chose you among your peers and more qualified people is not an accident. It has been his divine plan for you to be a co-labourer with him at his place of work. Rejoice in your calling; work hard at your duty post.

Should the storms of life want to shake your faith, remember he that called you is faithful and will keep you from falling. Should discouragements come your way, remember your labour is not in vain. Should the glory of the world want to distract you, remember the glory awaiting you far outweighs all of them combined. What better glory can you sacrifice and work for?

God is able to keep you standing strong where he posted you. Keep standing on his promises, even when the environment where you work continues to be hard and hostile. It is bound to be. Remember Christ who sent you on this errand said he will always be with you (Matthew 28:20). May his grace abide with you for all seasons. May his joy remain your strength. We shall all soon "come rejoicing bringing in the sheaves."

Thank you for availing yourself to be God's workmanship prepared for good work.

Yours in him,
Namani J. Nharrel

For more free resources for missionaries, scan this code

ACKNOWLEDGEMENTS

I thank God who made it possible to write this account of faith. The work started towards the end of our stay in Kamukuland in 1999. However, the Lord helped me to keep revising and adding new material to the manuscript over time. This is the second printing after the first in 2020, under the title *Encouraged by Their Faith*.

I am grateful to my wife and friend, Laku, who has been a wonderful encouragement to me in ministry ever since we agreed to become missionaries during our courtship.

I am deeply touched by the support of two key men: Rev (Dr) David Abolarin, who was my immediate pastor at Evangelical Church Winning All (ECWA) Bacita, Kwara State, from where my wife and I left for missions, and Mr Chimezie Onyebilanma, my missionary colleague and friend.

Although I did not inform him early enough, Rev Abolarin made the church pray for my family and released us to work with Calvary Ministries (CAPRO). He is a very humble man. While in Bacita, he encouraged our outreach to Bode Sadu where my family and Sha'aibu Shigben Isa planted a church among some migrant farmers (Dakarkari, Kambari, and Dukawa) from Kebbi and Niger states; and to some fishing settlements of Zabarmawa people from Kebbi State along the river Niger. I recall my wife and I visiting Rev Abolarin's family from our mission field. By then, he had moved to Ilorin to become the ECWA Ilorin District Church Council (DCC) Secretary. When we alighted from the taxi, he came and carried our heavy travelling bag on his head to the house. After that visit, we lost contact. I reconnected with him via phone call about 16 years later, and he gave me the surprise of my life. "How is the mission field?" he asked. "I pray for you every Monday since you left Bacita," he revealed. Unknown to me, my pastor had lifted my family and ministry in prayer before the Lord for about 20 years!

Chimezie and I trained for mission work in set 27 at the CAPRO School of Mission, Gana Ropp. I call him my "running mate." Each of us came with about a six-month-old daughter. Before the year ended, we each had a second daughter. Our third and fourth children were boys born on mission fields. Chimezie introduced me to A. W. Tozer who became one of my favourite authors. He has been my accountability partner since our training days at Gana Ropp and after he left to work in Togo and South Africa. One day he wrote, "Nharrel, I pray for you every Wednesday since we left Gana Ropp."

I am surprised that God is using very busy ministers to pray consistently for me. But then I understand why, in spite of my weaknesses, God has used me thus far. Whatever God enabled us to do in Kamuku field and in mission work in general was in answer to the prayers of the likes of Rev David Abolarin and Chimezie Onyebilanma. Some we know and others we do not know. To God be the glory and praise. Should I and my wife receive credit at all, it would go to our prayer partners and supporters.

I thank all my co-labourers, those who pioneered the CAPRO work in Kamukuland in 1990 and teammates with whom we worked between 1996 and 2000 to see that Christ is enthroned in Kamukuland. My prayer is that the fruit of our collective labours will continue to flourish in Kamukuland and beyond until Jesus comes.

I thank all who helped to make the first edition of this book a reality. These include Professor Odebunmi Ezekiel Oluyemi who, in addition to writing the original preface, also took time to do some editorial work on the book. Mr Ralph Madugu, editor of *Today's Challenge* magazine, and Eric Pam of the English department in Plateau State Polytechnic in

Nigeria, helped with editing. Miss Uche Ofulue proofread and did more editorial work. Several others read through and made corrections and useful suggestions.

Mrs Nora Okoye saw the title of the book listed among my works in *His Commands in Other Words* (one of my published books), and without knowing or meeting me in person, offered to contribute financially to the first edition's printing. Pastor Sunny Wogu of the Redeemed Christian Church of God gave money for its production. Mr Erasmus and Dr Mary Sulai made a donation after the latter went through the book and did corrections. I am very grateful to these and others who gave towards the realization of this work, but whose names are not mentioned here, because the book was already with the printer when their contributions came in.

I thank Yammune, my daughter and the only strong critic I have had so far. She read the final draft and pointed out many lapses – that some stories were too scattered to follow while others were scanty.

Now in my second printing and under a new title, I wish to thank my wonderful editors. Miss Hannah Rasmussen, the acquisitions editor at Oasis International Publishing has been very encouraging. Not only did she consider the book worth publishing, she also made useful suggestions as we worked together on this new and international edition.

Thanks to the publishers at Oasis International who have agreed to publish this book even if the writer is not a well-known author.

Mrs Tabitha Crowley of SIM has been very wonderful at re-editing the book to suit the publishers' specifications. As we worked together on this edition, I find her a very considerate, friendly, and caring person. I appreciate all her valuable contributions in making this book what it is in its present form.

Apart from those who came alongside me in ensuring the book came to be, there are those without whom the stories themselves would not have happened.

I thank the Kamuku believers whose lives provided the amazing stories recorded here, and many more that are not written down. For good reasons, I have changed their names. These believers agreed for me to write their stories and supplied vital details, including historical events that occurred before I arrived in the land and after I left. I am indebted to these wonderful believers whose faith encouraged mine, and I believe will encourage that of the readers.

I received encouragement from many individuals and churches who believed in and supported our work faithfully and sacrificially. Some visited to encourage us with their presence and presents. Worthy of mention is the Ilorin Chapter, now Ilorin CAST (CAPRO Sending Team), in financing many of the projects we undertook. The members contributed much in putting up buildings on the field, and I consider them wonderful teammates.

I must also appreciate the hand of fellowship extended to us by Christian denominations such as the Baptist Church and the United Missionary Church for Africa (UMCA), which were in Kamukuland long before Calvary Ministries (CAPRO) entered to work in the Tegina, Maruba, Kaya, Ukuru, and Uchindawa areas. The Baptist pastors in Mariga and Kagara assisted in our field activities, such as teaching in the Discipleship Training School (DTS). I was humbled by Mr Bahago, the UMCA pastor in Kampanin Bobi, who submitted himself to participate in the DTS with some of his church members. He studied at the school during the week and returned to minister in his church on weekends.

The ECWA Church, Lemu Road, in Kaduna supported our work, and even after leaving the field they still consider my wife and me as their missionaries. The same goes for the Chapel of Grace, Obafemi Awolowo University Teaching Hospital (OAUTH) Complex, whose support continued long after we left Kamuku. I recall one of its pastors, my friend Adesegun Fatusi, visiting us in Kangon Biri and appreciating what he saw. I asked him if he was going to join us on the mission field, and he replied, "No! But I now know how to go and pray appropriately for mission work."

I thank all the partners – individuals, churches, and organizations – who prayed, gave, visited, and aided the Kamuku work in one way or the other. Without you, Kamukuland would not have heard the gospel in the way it did, and these stories would not have come to pass to be written.